GENERATION ALT®

THE NEW MOVEMENT IN ALTERNATIVE INVESTING

Clifford Jack

FT Press

Associate Publisher: Amy Neidlinger
Operations Specialist: Jodi Kemper
Cover Designer: Chuti Prasertsith
Managing Editor: Kristy Hart
Senior Project Editor: Lori Lyons
Proofreader: Katie Matejka
Indexer: Tim Wright
Compositor: Gloria Schurick
Manufacturing Buyer: Dan Uhrig

© 2015 by Jack Clifford
Pearson Education, Inc.
Publishing as FT Press
Upper Saddle River, New Jersey 07458

This book is sold with the understanding that neither the author nor the publisher is engaged in rendering legal, accounting, or other professional services or advice by publishing this book. Each individual situation is unique. Thus, if legal or financial advice or other expert assistance is required in a specific situation, the services of a competent professional should be sought to ensure that the situation has been evaluated carefully and appropriately. The author and the publisher disclaim any liability, loss, or risk resulting directly or indirectly, from the use or application of any of the contents of this book.

For information about buying this title in bulk quantities, or for special sales opportunities (which may include electronic versions; custom cover designs; and content particular to your business, training goals, marketing focus, or branding interests), please contact our corporate sales department at corpsales@pearsoned.com or (800) 382-3419.

For government sales inquiries, please contact governmentsales@pearsoned.com.

For questions about sales outside the U.S., please contact international@pearsoned.com.

Company and product names mentioned herein are the trademarks or registered trademarks of their respective owners.

All rights reserved. No part of this book may be reproduced, in any form or by any means, without permission in writing from the publisher.

Printed in the United States of America

First Printing July 2014

Paperback:
ISBN-10: 0-13-339190-6
ISBN-13: 978-0-13-339190-9

Hardcover:
ISBN-10: 0-13-375605-X
ISBN-13: 978-0-13-375605-0

Pearson Education LTD.
Pearson Education Australia PTY, Limited.
Pearson Education Singapore, Pte. Ltd.
Pearson Education Asia, Ltd.
Pearson Education Canada, Ltd.
Pearson Educación de Mexico, S.A. de C.V.
Pearson Education—Japan
Pearson Education Malaysia, Pte. Ltd.

Paperback: Library of Congress Control Number: 2014937251
Hardback: Library of Congress Control Number: 2014937252

Jackson National Life Distributors LLC

Contents at a Glance

	Foreword x
One	What Goes Up... 1
Two	The Modern Portfolio Problem 9
Three	A Volatile Reality 19
Four	It's a Smaller World After All................. 31
Five	Disappearing Diversification 43
Six	Exploring the Alternative Universe............ 55
Seven	Play the Percentages 67
Eight	Beta Blockers 77
Nine	Think Outside the Style Box 89
Ten	The Scouting Report 99
Eleven	Survival of the Fittest....................... 107
Twelve	Fast and Furious............................ 115
Thirteen	How Leverage Works....................... 125
Fourteen	Over the Hedge 133
Fifteen	Strategy and Execution 145
Sixteen	Completing the Picture 157
	Glossary.................................... 163
	Index 173

Contents

	Foreword x
One	What Goes Up.... 1
Two	The Modern Portfolio Problem 9
	The Long and Winding Road: Preparing for the Ride 11
	Employers Stall Out: Finding a New Map to Your Financial Future 14
	From the Alt Vault: Valuable Takeaways from Chapter Two 18
Three	A Volatile Reality 19
	Motion Sickness: Markets Are Increasingly Cyclical 20
	Investor Shock: When Fear Leads to Missed Opportunities 25
	New Prescription: Rethink Buy-and-Hold 27
	Is It Time to See a Specialist? The Role of Proper Diversification 28
	Radical Idea: Do Something Different 29
	From the Alt Vault: Valuable Takeaways from Chapter Three 29
Four	It's a Smaller World After All 31
	Booster Shot: Globalization Begins 33
	Immune System Breakdown: Volatility Reaches Fever Pitch 35
	Modern Medicine: Combating Home Country Bias 36
	Second Opinion: The Best Advisors Seek the Counsel of Their Peers 38
	Fatal Mistake: Do Nothing 40
	From the Alt Vault: Valuable Takeaways from Chapter Four 40
Five	Disappearing Diversification 43
	Sugary Sweet: Learning Self-Control 45
	Similar Taste: The Rise of Correlation 46

	Proper Diversification: A Well-Balanced Diet 51
	Thirst for Diversification: Develop an All-Weather Strategy. 51
	From the Alt Vault: Valuable Takeaways from Chapter Five. 53
Six	**Exploring the Alternative Universe. 55**
	Flight Plan: Collaborate to Win 56
	Down to Earth: What It Means for the Average Investor . . . 60
	Alternative Investments: No Longer So Alien 62
	From the Alt Vault: Valuable Takeaways from Chapter Six. 65
Seven	**Play the Percentages 67**
	Risk Mitigation: Eye on the Ball 68
	Loss Aversion: Play It Safe. 69
	Hall of Fame: Unparalleled Returns. 71
	From the Alt Vault: Valuable Takeaways from Chapter Seven 75
Eight	**Beta Blockers 77**
	The Prescription: Bringing Balance 78
	Better Beta: Reduce Stress 81
	Clinical Trial: Safe for Public Use? 83
	Risk Parity 86
	From the Alt Vault: Valuable Takeaways from Chapter Eight. 87
Nine	**Think Outside the Style Box 89**
	Boxing Out: A Defensive Strategy. 90
	Xs and Os: Running a New Play 93
	Driving the Lane: The Importance of (Timely and Consistent) Yield 95
	From the Alt Vault: Valuable Takeaways from Chapter Nine 97
Ten	**The Scouting Report 99**
	Due Diligence: A Fundamental Layup. 101
	Size and Reach: Is Bigger Better? 102
	Team Performance: Stars vs. Cellars 103

	Preparation: The REIT Way to Do It 103
	Expensive Egos: Managing the Managers 104
	From the Alt Vault: Valuable Takeaways from Chapter Ten 105
Eleven	**Survival of the Fittest** **107**
	Hedge Funds: Asset Hunters and Gatherers and More 109
	Alternative Investments: Global Migration Patterns 111
	From the Alt Vault: Valuable Takeaways from Chapter Eleven 113
Twelve	**Fast and Furious** **115**
	Post-Modern Portfolios: Revving the Engine 117
	Getting Tactical: Rotate the Tires 118
	Alternative Investments: Riding an Annuity Chassis 120
	Portfolio Optimization: Balancing Risk and Return 122
	Portfolio Overlay: Understanding the Diagnostics 122
	From the Alt Vault: Valuable Takeaways from Chapter Twelve 123
Thirteen	**How Leverage Works** **125**
	The Mortgage Industry: Strawberry Fields Forever 127
	130/30 Funds: Short But Growing Longer 128
	Leverage: Note the Danger and Look Down 129
	From the Alt Vault: Valuable Takeaways from Chapter Thirteen 131
Fourteen	**Over the Hedge** **133**
	Hedge Funds 135
	Partnerships 139
	Liquidity and Alternatives 141
	From the Alt Vault: Valuable Takeaways from Chapter Fourteen 143
Fifteen	**Strategy and Execution** **145**
	Relative Value 149
	Event-Driven 151
	Equity L/S 152

	Global Macro 153
	Multi-Strategy 155
	From the Alt Vault: Valuable Takeaways from Chapter Fifteen 155
Sixteen	**Completing the Picture** **157**
	So What Now? 159
	10 Important Points to Remember 159
	Glossary **163**
	Index **173**

Acknowledgments

I would like to extend my thanks and appreciation to the following people who have contributed to the creative and technical development of this project: Larissa Agazzi, Mary Aragon, Katie Carney (Cover Art and Graphics), Sasha Franger, Mark Godfrey, Luis Gomez, DeAnna Hemmings, Rick Catts, Amy McIntosh, Diane Montana, Jeremy Rafferty, Danny Rubin (Illustrations), Kezia Samuel, Taylor Short, Daniel Starishevsky, John Sullivan, Stephanie Visscher, Tom Wald, Daniel Wright, and C. Philip Wright.

About the Author

CLIFFORD JACK
Head of Retail
Jackson National Life Insurance Company®

With nearly three decades of experience in the financial field, Clifford Jack, author of *Generation Alt: The New Movement in Alternative Investing*, currently serves as the head of retail for Jackson®. He also takes charge of the company's corporate growth initiatives. One that he feels especially passionate about is alternatives.

With the blurring of lines between international and domestic markets and world-wide political, social, and economic uncertainty, Jack feels strongly that investors need a strategic approach to investing amid a turbulent global economy. "Empowering investors and their advisors with knowledge about alternatives is the purpose of this book," says Jack. "I want my readers to understand the risks involved, but also show them the compelling reasons they should consider tapping into the powerful potential of alternatives."

Jack graduated from San Francisco State University. He resides in Colorado with his family.

Foreword

By Matt Botein, Chief Investment Officer & Co-Head, Blackrock Alternative Investors

For decades, people were taught that the basics of investing were simple—you built up your portfolio with a mix of stocks and bonds, adjusting the mix according to your age and tolerance for risk. And for years this was, in fact, the right idea—or at least right enough.

Then came the gut punch of the 2007 financial crisis. Since then, we've had to relearn everything we *thought* we knew. One tough lesson: Relying solely on a mix of stocks and bonds in a portfolio might not be enough anymore.

Unprecedented low yields, equities that seemed detached from fundamentals, bouts of volatility, and a high correlation between asset classes during periods of market distress have all made it tremendously challenging for investors to get the returns or consistent income they need from a traditionally constructed portfolio.

It's not that the risk-focused investment principles developed decades ago have been discredited, rather, it's that today's investment landscape requires a different approach to risk—a different way of thinking about risk, and thus a different set of tools to address it.

For many investors, "alternatives" are the new tools for building portfolios that can help meet today's challenges.

Alternative investments don't necessarily have a lot in common, they just happen *not* to be long-only stocks, bonds, or cash. But that's the point. Understanding the differences between asset classes is part of the reason for investing in alts in the first place—that is, finding growth opportunities and effectively managing risk when other parts of the market are all more or less moving in the same direction. The possibilities are many: long/short, hedge funds, private equity, real estate, commodities, and more.

But awareness of the wide range of options available is only part of alternative investing.

Understanding how they can fit in a portfolio—how they complement other holdings, what they do to your risk and return profiles—is equally crucial.

Enter *Generation Alt*.

The book you have before you doesn't just provide information about the different alternative asset classes. Cliff Jack gives you a strategy for how to understand these investments and the ways that investors can engage with them.

It's important for investors to consider some key questions: how to select the right manager, how to allocate between different alternative assets, and how to adjust those allocations. *Generation Alt* provides readers with important insight into these questions.

This book also provides critical lessons for today's markets that any investor in any asset class could benefit from—learning how to recognize the outdated strategies or assets in your portfolio, the effects of volatility and globalization on your investments, and the "disappearing diversification" in today's markets. This last point is also a great insight into the *why* of alternative investing.

But it's not just the *why*—this is an actionable book. Cliff also tells you *how*. How to make the appropriate preparations if you decide to move into alts. How to balance risk and performance. How to think about the different tools available to alternatives investors.

Knowledge is power, and *Generation Alt* gives investors the knowledge and the confidence they need to make smart alternatives choices.

Use it well.

One
What Goes Up...

Did you hear the Dow is going to 36,000?

At least that's what James Glassman, former *Washington Post* columnist and Undersecretary of State to President George W. Bush, argued in his 1999 book, *Dow 36,000: The New Strategy for Profiting from the Coming Rise in the Stock Market.* Co-written with Kevin A. Hassett, the title hinted at a steep rise in the stock market within five years.[1] The Dow[SM], of course, refers to the Dow Jones Industrial Average[SM], a market barometer that measures the price-weighted average of 30 actively traded blue chip stocks.[2] As it turned out, the bull market Glassman and Hassett predicted ended up being a bubble that popped when the Dow hit 11,722.98 on January 14, 2000.[3] "One of my colleagues...told me to never tie the Dow to a specific date," Glassman said in an interview more than a decade later. "I wish I had gotten the advice sooner."[4]

---

[1] James K. Glassman and Kevin A. Hassett, Three Rivers Press, *DOW 36,000: The New Strategy for Profiting from the Coming Rise in the Stock Market*, 1999.

[2] All indices referenced herein are unmanaged and not available for direct investment. Please refer to the glossary for all index definitions.

[3] Jack Ulick, *CNN Money*, "Dow's Peak, 3 Years Later," January 14, 2003.

[4] John Sullivan, *AdvisorOne*, "Author James Glassman's Surprising Advice for Investment Success: The Weekend Interview," February 2011.

He was hardly alone. Consider similarly miscalculated statements made just before and during the economic downturn of 2008.

> "I expect there will be some failures...I don't anticipate any serious problems of that sort among the large, internationally active banks that make up a very substantial part of our banking system."
>
> —Federal Reserve Chairman Ben Bernanke, February 2008[5]

> "I think this is a case where Fannie and Freddie are fundamentally sound, that they are not in danger of going under...I think they are in good shape going forward."
>
> —House Financial Services Committee Chairman Barney Frank (D-Mass.), July 2008[6]

> "I'm not an economist, but I do believe that we're growing."
>
> —President George W. Bush at a press conference, July 2008[7]

So-called experts who try to predict market behavior seem to appear every time we find ourselves in the midst of an expansion or contraction we believe may never end. Some new innovation, global condition, political environment, or earth shattering event leads one to believe *it's different this time*—only to find out later, it wasn't.

In the wake of the global housing and market collapse of 2008, I've heard much the same—prepare for lower returns, global growth will be muted for the foreseeable future, economies will *bump along the bottom*,

---

[5] CNBC, Reuters and AP, CNBC.com, "Fed Chairman: Some Small U.S. Banks May Go Under," February 2008.

[6] John M. O'Hara, John Wiley & Sons, *A New American Tea Party*, 2010.

[7] Office of the Press Secretary, The White House of President George W. Bush, "Press Conference by the President," July 2008.

and recovery will be a *long, slow slog*. But while the benefit of hindsight makes it easy to scoff at predictions of market cycles past, is it truly different this time? I would say, yes and no.

Too many investors make the mistake of believing that each market boom or bust necessitates a complete change in investment strategy, but this is rarely the case. Rather, simple adjustments could help stabilize a portfolio. In fact, the theories of modern investing pioneer Harry Markowitz, whom I will discuss at length throughout this book, have been used for decades in all sorts of market climates. His frameworks are constant, they just require new inputs. Think of it this way: the science (framework) behind Ford's Model-T doesn't much differ from cars today. Fuel powers a combustion engine that causes four tires to rotate. But new efficiencies and features (variables) developed in recent decades mean cars can set out for destinations in all kinds of conditions and on all kinds of terrain.

To continue the metaphor, different investment strategies have been developed to help navigate any number of terrains. While there is always risk of losing money, access is available to strategies that have been designed specifically to help minimize (or maximize) the impact of the terrain, depending on one's intention. For example, alternative investments, variable annuities, and hedge funds are all products that may help during a market shift. Each of these products will be defined at length in the chapters that follow, along with their potential risks. One of which, of course, is the loss of the investor's money.

Here's a little known fact about 2008. While the world was awash in economic chaos over fears that entire countries could go under, when the populace panicked, and almost every sector seemed to be down,[8] several alternative and fixed income indices fared better than traditional equity indices. Focusing on alternative indices, while many alternative indices were down, several of these indices performed better than the overall

---

[8] Department of the Treasury, "Recent U.S. Economic Growth in Charts," May 2012.

market (as measured by the Russell 3000 Index).[9] For this analysis, I examined the performance of 17 separate indices, including alternative indices, equity indices, and fixed income indices that I used as a proxy for asset classes. It is important to know that indices are not available for direct investment.

Although in existence for decades, the increasing interest and strategic use of alternative investments in this new economic environment is the catalyst for what I've termed "Generation Alt—The New Movement in Alternative Investing."

Generation Buy and Hold, what I would call the prior cohort, carried the flag for years thanks to strong overall economic growth and steadily lowering interest rates. Unfortunately, very little of what happened then looks like the post-2008 markets of today. In fact, after the meltdown, investors in Generation Buy and Hold quickly became Generation Buy and Fold, exiting the market altogether to wait for signs of life—and some are still waiting. As of March 2013, investors were still sitting on $9.81 trillion in cash and cash equivalents (which comprised of money market mutual funds, money market deposit accounts, and small-denomination time deposits).[10]

Enter Generation Alt, a new era of investors who understand that time is money and that heading to the sidelines to escape volatility will not help to achieve their long-term goals. I think they need an investment strategy that helps them stay invested no matter how markets perform. Alternative investments may be one possibility to help investors do just that.

Defined as anything other than stocks, bonds, or cash that may increase or decrease independently of traditional securities (think hedge funds, managed futures, real estate, and commodities), alternative investments

---

[9] Lipper, a Thomson Reuters Company, Downloaded April 2013.

[10] Compiled by Peter Crane, Crane Data, using Federal Reserve Data, March 2013.

have the potential to help manage the dual problems of increasing correlation and lack of portfolio diversification.

Although far from a simple one-size-fits-all strategy, alternative investments can play a role in day-to-day investment portfolios by helping to provide diversification in an increasingly globalized and homogenized investment world. Even though they've existed for years, I believe alternative investments, combined with new philosophies, are positioned to be the next disruptive movement in the ongoing evolution of the investment management and financial services industries.

Disruption, in this context, is a term that refers to any idea that overturns convention, questions assumptions, and takes steps toward a new future.[11] At first they seem of limited interest, but eventually their ideas catch on and can encourage new thinking. Look at how the advent of MP3 technology and iPods completely changed the way we listen to and purchase music. Not only did songs become available for download, but it also sparked a movement to other forms of digital content—movies, TV shows, and books. The status quo, at one point a boom box or Sony Walkman, was disrupted. While I am not suggesting that alternative investments are the iPod of alternative investing, they may become an unexpected disruption in financial services due to a need for more diversification in the face of increasingly correlated markets—something we will discuss at length. With increased accessibility and education, I believe that alternative investments, or alts, have the potential to help investors navigate market uncertainty.

At the core of this uncertainty is volatility, or the sharp rise and fall in price within a short-term period. What's creating it? I could point to several things. The blurring of investment lines internationally means investors can now quickly react to political and economic events worldwide. I've witnessed the effects of technology on the speed of investing, and not always to the benefit of the investor. While technology can be

---

[11] Luke Williams, Pearson Education, *Disrupt*, 2011.

liberating, it can also, in my mind, create problems that did not exist as recently as 20 years ago.

Things like flash trading, day trading, and frequency trading have had an impact on sound investment structures and contribute to the manic markets we now experience. I would argue that in our increasingly interconnected world, dampening volatility absolutely makes sense. In 2008, it became evident that alternative investments might well be the right strategy for this volatile environment. How so? In contrast to the overall market drop, university endowments, for example, fared better during the economic downturn. Their "secret" was their use of alternative investments. I don't mean to imply that endowments had gains in 2008, I am only pointing out that endowments fared better. And it is important to remember that while alternatives and endowments do not always outperform the market (as we saw in 2012), they certainly fared better during the most recent downturn. Most recently, in the year ended June 2013, endowments did slightly decrease their allocation to alts to 47% of their portfolio and returns were an average of 11.7% in one year.[12]

Long available to qualified, high-net-worth investors, they were little known to average retail investors outside of Wall Street wirehouse firms and the aforementioned universities. In fact, average retail investors, those investing for their own benefit (retirement, their kid's college, etc.), still do not have access to exactly the same investments as endowments—yet alternative investments are now attracting the attention of these smaller investors for a number of reasons, which I will discuss. But perhaps the biggest is the increase in recent years in market correlation and volatility, twin concepts that figure prominently in the relative success and failure of any investment portfolio.

---

[12] Overall market measured by S&P 500: Lipper, a Thomson Reuters Company, 2013; Endowments: NACUBO, National Association of College and University Business Officers and Commonfund Institute, "Commonfund Study of Endowments," 2013; Tim Sturrock, *FundFire*, "Endowment Returns Strong, Alt Allocations Drop," November 7, 2013.

Think of it this way: It took 76 years for the Dow Jones Industrial Average to close above 1,000 on November 14, 1972, less than half that time to rise 1,300% to its pre-crisis high of 14,000 on July 19, 2007,[13] and just 18 months to lose *more than half its value* to close at 6,547.05 on March 9, 2009.[14] Our increasingly interconnected world means that if current trends continue, this type of compression in reaching market milestones, and the volatility that drives it, will likely increase.[15] While 100-point swings in daily market performance are not unheard of, today they're far too common.[16] The lack of volatility in an investment portfolio may be a way to measure financial "success," however, individuals, couples, families, or even foundations may have different tolerances when it comes to volatility.

As baby boomers retire, they may have the greatest need to access the full universe of available investments. Should another crisis appear, they no longer have time to wait for a rebound before drawing on their financial resources for retirement. By understanding the benefits of investment strategies with low correlations to traditional markets, I believe investors have a good chance of hedging against the same problems experienced in 2008. Throughout the book, we will explore how alternative investments were developed. We'll also look at the success they experienced in the past, how the investment market has changed, and discuss why alternatives may be worth considering.

---

[13] Brendan McDermid, *The Washington Post*, "The History of the Dow Jones Industrial Average," March 2013; djaverages.com, "Dow Jones Industrial Average Milestones," July 2012.

[14] Alexandra Twin, *CNN Money*, "For Dow, Another 12-year Low," March 2009.

[15] Judith Rodin and Robert Garris, *USAID*, "Reconsidering Resilience for the 21st Century," June 2012.

[16] Samuel H. Williamson, *MeasuringWorth*, "Daily Closing Value of the Dow Jones Average, 1885 to Present," 2013.

Additionally, we'll answer a number of important questions, including:

- How are alternative investments defined and how do they differ from traditional investments?
- What is meant by high and low correlation?
- How did alternative investments develop and what benefits have certain investors realized from their use?
- What are the different types of alternative investments and what role do they play in investing?
- What situations involving alternative investments should be carefully considered?
- What impact can alternatives have on volatility and performance over the long term?

As I mentioned, a new movement is afoot—one focused on alternative investments that can alter the way people invest. I call it *Generation Alt*. The concepts detailed in *Generation Alt* are specifically designed to explain the increased globalization and the hyper-connectivity of today's markets, and the volatility all of it brings.

Let's discuss...

Two

The Modern Portfolio Problem

Is that an Eldorado parked in your portfolio?

I f only it were just a car.

The 1959 Cadillac Eldorado "isn't so much a car as a cathedral," writes automobile guru Quentin Willson.[17] Innovative, cool, rich, and stylish, it came to epitomize America's post-war swagger. With its space-age style, 390 cubic inch V8 engine and—of course—those fins. "The most telling thing about the '59 is its sheer in-yer-face arrogance," according to Willson. But the car's attitude, like the country's, would soon sputter. By the mid-1960s, the country was mired in war, divided culturally, and in the midst of a serious crisis of national confidence. While the Eldorado captured a moment and was, for its time, the essence of modern, it quickly faded. "A decade of glitz, glamour, and prosperity was coming to an end," Willson concludes. "America would never be the same again, and neither would her Cadillacs."

Standards are set to be changed. Modern becomes old. And while it is easy to spot an old classic like the Cadillac Eldorado on the road today, it is not so easy for people to spot an outdated investment model. In other words, you may have a brand new SUV in your garage, but it's possible you still have an Eldorado parked in your portfolio.

Modern Portfolio Theory, or MPT, was first developed by Harry Markowitz in 1952.[18] MPT is a theory of finance that attempts to maximize return for a given level of risk. Although revolutionary at the time (for which Markowitz was awarded a Nobel Prize) and a popular strategy of investing for more than 50 years, some of its basic assumptions have been challenged in recent years, especially in the wake of the economic crisis of 2008. It's not that I think that the theory itself is flawed, rather, it's that the nature of investing has changed—and changed greatly. As a result, even long-held beliefs have been tested.

Somewhere along the way, investors have been encouraged to "set it and forget it"—to pick a rudimentary asset allocation, glance at their

---

[17] Quentin Willson, DK Publishing, "Classic American Cars," 1997.

[18] Harry M. Markowitz, Nobel Prize, *Autobiography*, 1990.

quarterly statements, and then file them away. Some have also been taught to rely on that simplistic notion of using their age as the basis of calculating the percentage of their portfolio allocated to fixed income, with the rest going to equities. For example, if they are 30 years old, 30% goes to bonds, with the remaining 70% allocated to equities. As they approach retirement, they begin to increase the amount of their allocation to bonds, resulting in a more conservative portfolio that is historically recommended for retirement. Traditionally, despite dips along the way, the stock market always increased over time, so why worry?

In today's increasingly fast-paced and interconnected world, such "rules of thumb" may be more harm than help. Those who fail to keep pace with change invariably fall victim to it—and find themselves left behind. Furthering our analogy, when looking under the hood of that vintage Cadillac, the engine may no longer be suitably equipped. And regardless of whether you are investing or driving, there are always associated risks that need to be carefully considered.

The Long and Winding Road: Preparing for the Ride

Before we drive ahead, let's take a quick look in the rearview mirror. At the core of the need for portfolio reconstruction is longevity. For the most part, we are living longer lives than we used to. At the start of the 20th century the average life expectancy was 47.3 years.[19] Yet in the next century alone, it lengthened by an additional 63%, due largely to sharp advances in medicine and medical technology.[20] In 2000, the average life expectancy at birth for a person born in the United States was 76.8 years, it was projected to be 78.3 years in 2010, and by 2020 it's predicted to be 79.5 years.[21] (See Figure 2.1.)

---

[19] U.S National Center for Health Statistics, "Health, United States, 2011, Table 22," 2011.

[20] Frank Lichtenberg, Columbia University and National Bureau of Economic Research, "The Impact of Biomedical Innovation on Longevity and Health," August 2012.

[21] U.S. Census Bureau, Statistical Abstract of the United States: 2012, "Table 104. Expectation of Life at Birth, 1970 to 2008, and Projections 2010 to 2020," 2012.

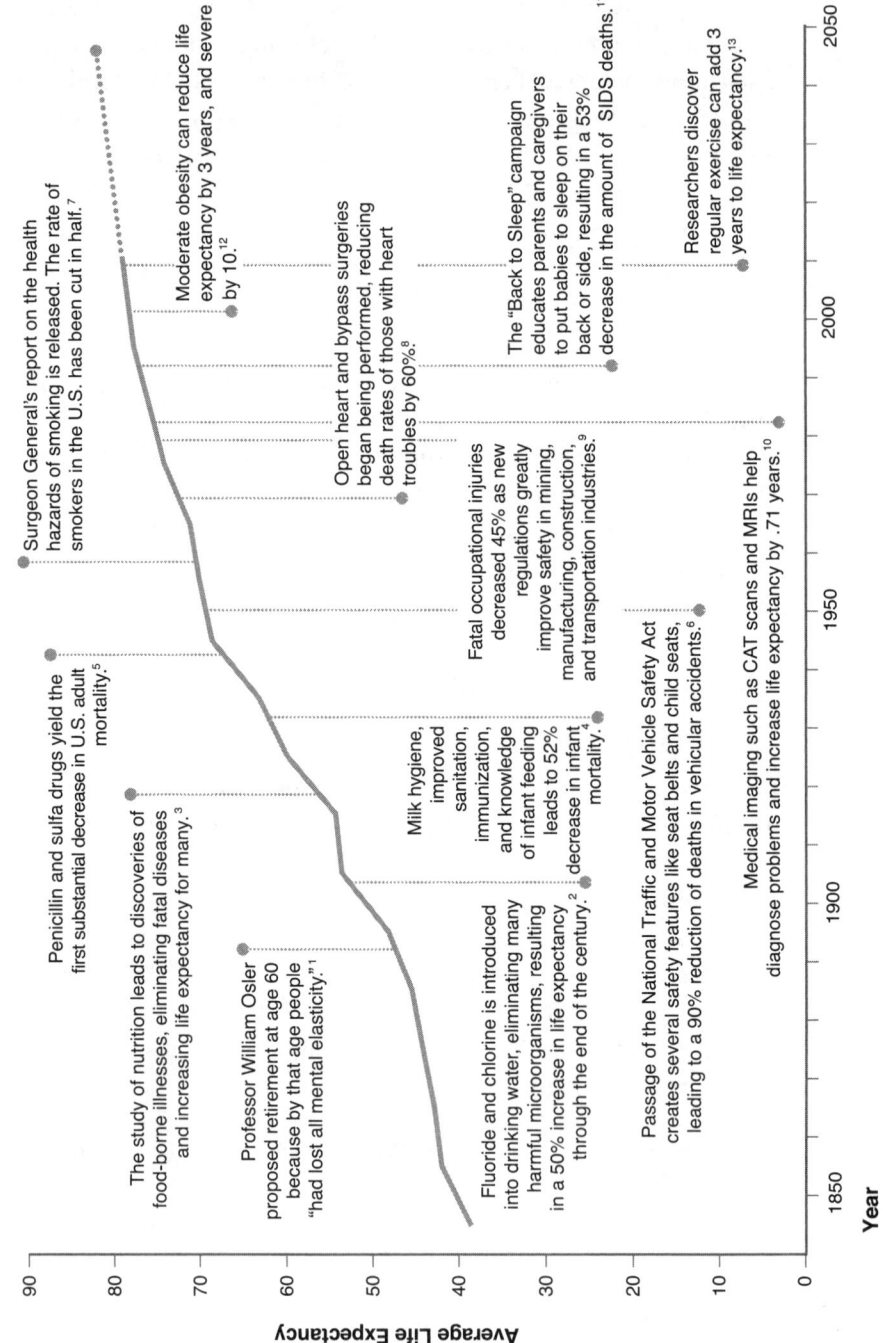

12   Generation Alt

Figure 2.1

Chart Sources:

1. Alex J. Pollock, American Enterprise Institute for Public Policy Research, "Retirement Finance: Old Ideas, New Reality," September 2006.

2. Chlorine Chemistry Council, "Chlorine and Drinking Water: Here's to Your Health," November 1995; Jamie Knotts, National Drinking Water Clearinghouse, "A Brief History of Drinking Water Regulations," 1999.

3. Centers for Disease Control, "Achievements in Public Health, 1900-1999," May 2001.

4. Centers for Disease Control, "What Is Public Health? The 20th Century's Ten Great Public Health Achievements in the United States," 2012.

5. Population Research Bureau, Research Highlights in the Demography and Economics of Aging, "The Future of Human Life Expectancy: Have We Reached the Ceiling or Is the Sky the Limit?" March 2006.

6. Centers for Disease Control, "Achievements in Public Health 1900-1999 Motor-Vehicle Safety: A 20th Century Public Health Achievement," 1999.

7. Maggie Fox, NBC News, "50 Years of Progress Cuts Smoking Rates in Half—But Can We Ever Get to Zero?" January 11, 2014.

8. Jim Atkinson, Esquire, "The Future of Your Heart Attack," 2013.

9. Centers for Disease Control, Morbidity & Mortality Weekly Report, "Fatal Occupational Injuries—United States, 1980-1997," April 2001.

10. Dr. Frank Lichtenberg, National Bureau of Economic Research, "Study Demonstrates Significant Increases in Life Expectancy Due to Advanced Medical Imaging," June 2009.

11. United States Department of Health & Human Services, "Preventing Infant Mortality," January 2006.

12. National Institutes of Health, NIH News, "Obesity Threatens to Cut U.S. Life Expectancy, New Analysis Suggests," March 2005.

13. Associated Press, MSNBC, "Exercise Can Add 3 Years to Life Expectancy," November 2005.

A lot has been written about longevity's impact on retirement. In my experience, retirement discussions used to revolve around it being a period of "short rest then death" after a lifetime of hard work. However, as life expectancy has increased, the traditional ideas of retirement have transformed. According to gerontologist Dr. Ken Dychtwald, today's retirees are looking forward to not to just a few remaining, peaceful years, but to an active lifestyle full of travel, second careers, more education, and perhaps even new romances. "People have...had enough chances to watch people play out their retirement to see what happens..." Dychtwald told *Investment Advisor* in late 2011. "For high-energy, stimulated, and stimulating people, retirement is boring... They've looked at their retired relatives and said, 'That's not for me.'"[22]

How could living longer and more fulfilling lives possibly be a problem? It's quite simple: How will we pay for it?

Employers Stall Out: Finding a New Map to Your Financial Future

The primary retirement plan for Americans used to be a defined benefit plan, one that promised a specified monthly amount of money upon retirement. Chances are your parents or grandparents (or someone you know) had a defined benefit plan. Simply put, they worked for a set period of time and were then periodically paid a set amount of money for the rest of their life. It might have come in the form of an exact dollar amount, such as $1,000 per month. Or, more commonly, the payment was calculated by using a formula that considers such factors as salary, length of service, and life expectancy.

---

[22] John Sullivan, *Investment Advisor*, "Retirement Reset," November 2011.

However, the Revenue Act of 1978 created the 401(k), a type of defined contribution plan, by removing payroll taxes on money that was deferred for a later payout.[23] Advantages of defined contribution plans included greater control, investment choice, and portability from one job to the next for employees, as well as lower associated costs for employers than defined benefit plans.[24] Over time, defined benefit plans faded in popularity and were replaced by defined contribution plans (see Figure 2.2). In 1980, the year the Revenue Act went into effect, almost 66% of private sector workers participated in defined benefit pension plans, while only 34% participated in defined contribution plans. By 2010, the numbers had flipped—68% of private sector workers participated in defined contribution plans while the number of private sector workers in defined benefit plans fell to 32%.[25] However, as with any investment program, defined contribution plans do not have the guaranteed payout often seen in pensions. As a result, more responsibility falls on investors interested in retirement planning to calculate how much they will need and to explore additional sources of income, if required.

---

[23] Employee Benefit Research Institute, "History of 401(k) Plans: An Update," February 2005.

[24] U.S. Bureau of Labor Statistics, Beyond the Numbers, "Retirement Costs for Defined Benefit Plans Higher Than for Defined Contribution Plans," December 2012.

[25] Employee Benefits Security Administration, U.S. Department of Labor, "Private Pension Plan Bulletin Historical Tables and Graphs," November 2012.

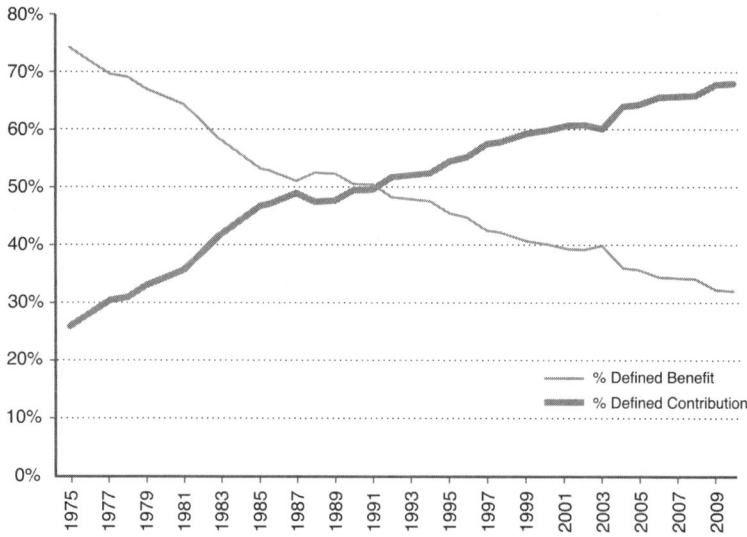

Chart created by Jackson National Life Insurance Company (Home office: Lansing, Michigan) utilizing data from U.S. Department of Labor, Employee Benefits Security Administration, Private Pension Plan Bulletin Historical Tables and Graphs, November 2012.

Figure 2.2

One common source of retirement income is, of course, Social Security. But longer life spans and the sheer size of the 78 million strong Baby Boomer generation (typically defined as those born between 1946 and 1964)[26] may be creating problems for the government program. The Social Security trust fund reserves are expected to run dry in 2033, after which income from taxes will be able to fund only three quarters of each benefit until 2086.[27] This leaves anyone planning to retire uncertain of how much, if any, Social Security income they will receive (see Figure 2.3).

---

[26] Daniel Luzer, *Washington Monthly*, "Old People More Likely to Be College Graduates," February 2012.

[27] Social Security and Medicare Boards of Trustees, "A Summary of the 2012 Annual Reports," April 2012.

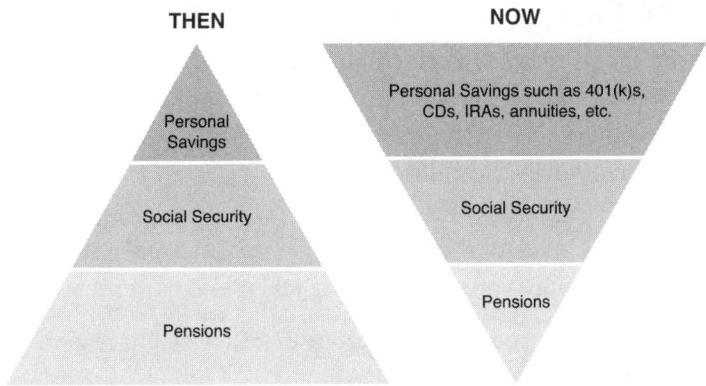

Chart created by Jackson National Life Insurance Company (Home office: Lansing, MI) using ideas from goasknewton.com, "Can We Count on the Three-Legged Stool?" 2013.

Figure 2.3

Throughout this book, I will do my best to illustrate why I think a portfolio model that includes alternatives may help investors in various market conditions and is thus worth considering. The term *diversification* in this sense is defined as the spreading of assets across different categories or industries. If the stock market rises or falls, alternative asset classes often move independently of both each other and traditional investments, helping to provide further diversification due to their independent characteristics.[28] While alternatives do not come without their own set of risks, the worldwide market collapse in 2008 offered few havens—especially in stocks, bonds, and other traditional investments. However, there is evidence that some alternative strategies may have fared better than some of their traditional counterparts. Alternative investments will not always outperform their traditional counterparts, but they may help manage volatility and the reaction to down markets. We will now turn to why.

---

[28] Diversification does not assure a profit or protect against a loss in a declining market. Portfolios that have a greater percentage of alternatives may have great risks, especially those including arbitrage, currency, leveraging, and commodities. This additional risk can offset the benefit of diversification.

From the Alt Vault: Valuable Takeaways from Chapter Two

Longer life spans, the transition from pension models, relying on Social Security, volatile markets, and investor self-reliance and confusion all add up to modern portfolio problems in search of more options. A new movement has taken shape—Generation Alt.

- Portfolios need to be periodically reviewed to make sure old and new investing strategies are being taken into account.
- Pensions are products of a bygone era. Retirement responsibility now falls on the individual.
- Increasing life spans mean increasing costs to companies. Defined Contribution plans are now the norm.
- Many financial services companies are taking a closer look at the strategic use of alternative investments to aid a new generation of investors and retirees.

What's next: Properly used, alternative investments historically reduced volatility and effected returns. The key phrase is *properly used*—but what, exactly, does that mean?

Three
A Volatile Reality

Is it time to adjust your sails?

Back when commercial air travel was still in its infancy and largely relegated to those who could afford it, steamship was the only option for many travelers. Few things were more miserable than falling ill at sea, especially if it was day one of a seven day voyage. Relief came in 1949, when dimenhydrinate, now widely marketed as Dramamine®, was introduced to the market.[29] For some travelers, this little pill (or patch) does wonders for helping to manage the nausea that accompanies high swells and angry seas. Just as a cruise ship unexpectedly encounters rough waters, the value of a portfolio can also experience sudden dips and dives that may leave investors queasy and ready for land. Yet, if you abandon ship at the first port you see, chances are you'll never reach your final destination.

While there is no known treatment to calm the nausea, anxiety, and other side effects involved with investing in a turbulent market, I believe alternatives can help, even though, as always, there are no assurances that they will. Let's face it; no one can control the ups and downs of the market, but when used in tandem with traditional investments, alternatives can help manage the volatility inside your portfolio, thereby reducing the spinning and dizziness you might feel and providing the needed confidence to finish the journey.

Motion Sickness: Markets Are Increasingly Cyclical

An office staple of many financial professionals during the nearly 20-year bull market from 1982 to 2000 was the S&P 500® chart detailing the rise of equities over the previous 70 years. Often prominently displayed as one would hang posters of fast cars and sports icons, it made for a colorful visual that framed nicely and illustrated that over time, despite fluctuations, markets trend up. That is, until one day they didn't.

---

[29] Encyclopedia Britannica, "Dimenhydrinate," 2013.

After the tech implosion at the beginning of the 2000, the S&P briefly wobbled and seemed to recover, only to find near catastrophic turbulence in 2008. From the perspective of a typical investor, experiencing the euphoria of a bull market and the despair of a bear market can feel like a ride on the proverbial emotional rollercoaster, as shown in Figure 3.1.

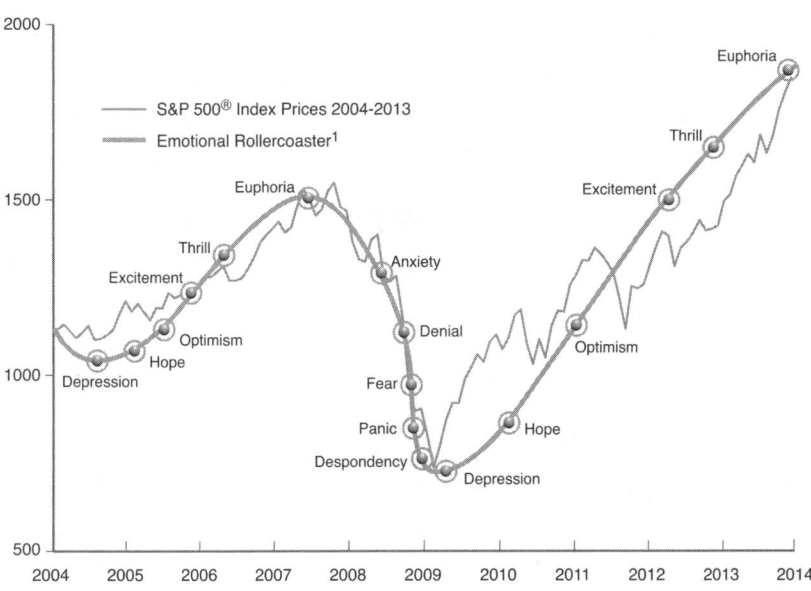

The S&P 500 Index is a market capitalization-weighted index of 500 stocks that are selected by Standard & Poor's to represent a broad array of large companies in leading industries. The S&P 500 Index is unmanaged and not available for direct investment. The payment of dividends is not reflected in the index return. S&P 500 Index monthly prices downloaded from Lipper, a Thomson Reuters Company, 2014.

[1] Jim Farrish, SeekingAlpha.com, "Managing Emotions is Essential to Money Management," October 22, 2010. Emotions plotted on chart were derived by Jackson National Life Insurance Company (Home office: Lansing, MI) from the theory developed in this article.

Figure 3.1

In the years since, the unpredictability of the market has continued. It used to behave in secular patterns (meaning over a long period of time) and could be fairly relied upon to allow for insight and planning. Today, it seems that cyclical volatility (or volatility occurring over a short period of time) is increasingly the norm. Since 2000, the adjective "rising" had been replaced by "sideways and volatile" when discussing market performance.

One index in particular is receiving an increase in scrutiny because of this increase in volatility. The Chicago Board Options Exchange (CBOE) Volatility Index®, or the VIX®, takes the average volatility for the Standard and Poor's 100 Index, which deals with futures (a contract to buy an asset at a predetermined price and future date), and uses it to measure the volatility of the overall market. A low VIX indicates investor confidence, while a high VIX indicates investor concern (some would say fear). For this reason it is informally referred to as the "fear index." Typically, a level of 30 or higher signals a great deal of volatility.[30] The VIX has reached a low of just below 10, while it hit almost 90 during the peak of the financial crisis in 2008. The long-term VIX average has been somewhere between 20 and 22.[31]

In the interest of examining history, I would argue that the roots of this volatility go back more than 30 years. There are several factors to consider in order to fully understand the unpredictability of a cyclical market. First, the secular decline of interest rates over the past three decades has had a significant influence on the U.S. economy and capital markets. If the economy dipped toward, or into, recession, the U.S. Federal Reserve, which controls short-term interest rates, would cut rates to spur a refinancing cycle and thus encourage economic activity.

As interest rates moved lower, consumers gained access to cheaper capital. The ability to refinance mortgages at lower rates every few years, for example, allowed individuals to reduce one of their most significant costs—that of their home. With data going back to the early 1990s, the average 30-year mortgage rate (as measured by Freddie Mac's Primary

---

[30] Investopedia, "CBOE - VIX," 2013.
[31] Macroption.com, "VIX Chart," 2013.

Mortgage Market Survey available on Freddie Mac's website and on Bloomberg) has gone from over 10% in the early 1990s to just above 4% by the end of the second quarter of 2013[32] (see Figure 3.2). This provided consumers with more disposable income to spend on other wants and needs.

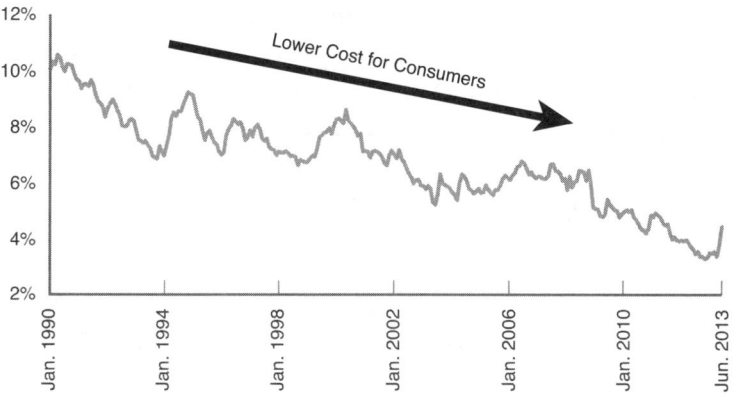

Figure 3.2

Business managers also enjoyed access to cheaper capital. Like homeowners, businesses were able to refinance their own debt or loan obligations at lower rates every few years, reducing their interest expense while increasing profits and helping to spur economic growth. Businesses have also been able to borrow at cheaper and cheaper costs, helping to expand their operations. The chart in Figure 3.3 shows the average yield of AAA-rated corporate bonds over the last 30 (plus) years. During this time period, their average yield for the highest-rated corporate bonds has dropped from a high of about 15.5% to around 4.3% at the end of the second quarter of 2013, using Moody's Seasoned Aaa Corporate Bond Yield Index.[33] Due in part to the lowering of interest rates during

---

[32] Bloomberg, "30-Year Fixed Rate Mortgage Index," January 1990–June 2013.

[33] Bloomberg, "AAA-Rated Corporate Bond Yields," December 1990–June 2013.

Chapter Three A Volatile Reality

the 20-year period between 1980 and 2000, the U.S. real gross domestic product (GDP) grew around 2.83% on average per year.[34]

Conversely, lower interest rates meant lower income from bonds available from the government. During this period of stock market growth, the 10-year U.S. Treasury yield went from its peak near 16% in 1981 to around 5% by the end of 2000.[35] In July 2012, the yield fell to a historic low of 1.47%. Now, however, lower interest rates seem to be losing their stimulus effect on the overall economy. In the years since 2001, the GDP has grown at a muted 1.75% average yearly rate.[36] Interest rates hit bottom, largely remained there since the economic crisis, and are now beginning to turn. As a result, the Fed is much more limited in how, and how much, it can stimulate the economy through refinancing. I believe this could result in more pronounced economic cycles, which in turn could influence a continued cyclical stock market pattern.

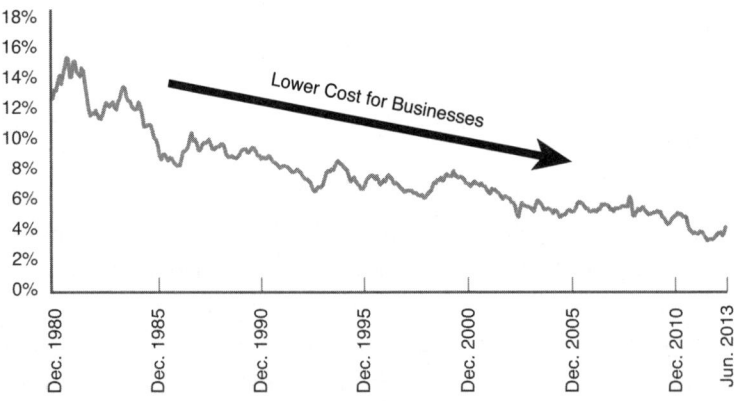

Chart created by Jackson National Life Insurance Company (Home office: Lansing, Michigan) utilizing data from Bloomberg. 12/31/1980–6/29/2013. Arrow added to show general direction.

Figure 3.3

---

[34] Bloomberg, "GDP Index," February 1980–December 2001.
[35] Bloomberg, "10-year U.S, Treasury Yield," December 1980–June 2013.
[36] Bloomberg, "GDP Index," March 2001–April 2013.

This means if the seismic trends experienced since 2008 continue, there could be more risk for a given level of return. And that, in turn, means a new approach may be needed to help manage that volatility. Unfortunately, too many people forget their Dramamine. Perhaps, they feel they can ride out whatever may come or, worse yet, they don't even know they're prone to seasickness. And so it is with their investments—they believe they can handle market volatility with traditional allocations, and may not even realize other options are available.

Investor Shock: When Fear Leads to Missed Opportunities

Undoubtedly, many investors were shell shocked when the stock market crashed in 2008; their investment portfolios took a significant hit and some thought it would be better to "cash out." But increased volatility means markets can quickly turn. If you're "on the sidelines" when that turn occurs, you could miss the eventual rally. For example, in 2009, despite many cyclical trends, the market appeared to generally move upwards. As a result, those who sold their investments missed an opportunity to regain some of what was lost.[37] To compound the problem, those investors who reentered the market largely did so by investing in fixed income assets such as bonds.[38]

I know of investors who relied on the standard 60/40 equities-to-fixed income split before the crisis who subsequently retreated to cash when the market crashed. These investors then flipped the ratio, significantly increasing their allocations to bonds, which in turn helped to drive bond yields (the potential returns generated) significantly lower. Money continued to pour into taxable bond funds until mid-2013, despite low interest rates and yields. The irony was that people were willing to invest in something that would earn them relatively lower returns

---

[37] Rebecca Lipman, Kapitall Wire, "Rallying Stocks: Will Small Investors Miss Out on the Rally, Again?," November 2011; Steven Reiff, *Advisor Today*, "Preparing Clients for New Market Realities," July/August 2012.

[38] Daniel Wagner, Yahoo Finance, "Bonds Retain Appeal, Despite Rock-Bottom Yields," August, 2012.

while, maybe unknowingly, exposing themselves to the risk that inflation would outpace their growth. The possibility of rising interest rates means fixed income vehicles are no longer as popular as they once were. Yet even though investors have materially changed their view of investing post crisis, I think it's the wrong view—especially if interest rates continue to rise.

Why? Many consumers might still retain the perception that their portfolios, allocated across a narrow spectrum of assets, will earn between 5% and 9% annually, something they might have experienced in earlier bull markets.[39] However, traditional fixed-income investments are susceptible to the pressures of increasing interest rates and inflation (yields have been historically low for the last few years,[40] which means investors are locking in low investment returns). And because the bond market has an inverse relationship with interest rates (low rates mean high prices, high rates mean low prices), the client's portfolio, heavy with fixed income allocations, may grow too slowly or be subject to increased bond market volatility. This could therefore cause the portfolio to be worth less at a time when principal and purchasing power is needed most—like, say, retirement. The point is that portfolio values increase and decrease over the life of the accumulation phase, but might be worth less at the exact moment investors need to begin withdrawing assets.

The goal of a retirement plan is to help investors accumulate enough assets during their working years to cover daily living expenses and any unexpected events that might arise in retirement, without severely depleting their savings. The importance of picking a broadly diversified investment allocation that fits with the investor's long-term needs can, therefore, not be overemphasized.

---

[39] Joseph Davis and Daniel Piquet, Vanguard Research, "Recessions and Balanced Portfolio Returns," October 2011.

[40] Federal Reserve, downloaded on 7/22/2013.

New Prescription: Rethink Buy-and-Hold

With so many factors now influencing a company's stock performance—especially in our increasingly globalized world—the days of relying on buy-and-hold investing, quite simply, may be days gone by. We've seen many once seemingly invincible companies fold due to unexpected (and unprepared for) circumstances. It was never a good idea to remain invested in a company over time simply for the sake of buy and hold. Today such strategies are especially dangerous. Here's an example of why:

Let's assume an analytical person, one who enjoys studying the underlying financials of companies and in-depth sector research, decides to buy Apple based upon its strong consumer brand. It's a traditional investment approach that relies completely on the financial fundamentals of a company, and one that until recently made sense. Today, however, it's just one aspect of a complex overall investment construct. Economic conditions that affect large markets such as China and Europe would certainly affect Apple's success. Apple employs many manufacturing workers through subsidiaries and sells many phones in China, so any increase or decrease in demand would affect the company's financial performance and, consequently, share price. In Europe, the sovereign debt crisis that recently spread throughout the continent increased the likelihood that financial institutions could face widespread write-downs, which would negatively affect shareholder returns.[41] This, in turn, increased the risk that the crisis would spread to markets in other parts of the world.[42] With all there is of which to keep track, how could the average investor possibly expect to sift through such macroeconomic information to determine the right time to buy or sell their individual Apple stock?

---

[41] Matthew Curtin, *The Wall Street Journal*, "Firms Brace for Write-Downs," January 2013.

[42] Katie Martin and Jonathan House, *The Wall Street Journal*, "Contagion Returns," February 2013.

Is It Time to See a Specialist? The Role of Proper Diversification

The result is that in today's world, it can be tough for individual investors to digest the incredible amount of information needed to make decisions about their portfolio. Institutions and endowments employ experts to strategically use alternative investments (among other types of investments) for the express purpose of capitalizing on, or managing, the effects of the types of scenarios described above. These strategies enable them to enjoy a broader range of diversification.[43] As I mentioned in the first chapter, since the downturn, endowment returns have been mixed. For their fiscal year that ended June 2012, endowment returns lagged those found in a traditional 60% equity/40% fixed income portfolio. However, for their fiscal year that ended June 2013, while allocations to alternatives decreased to 47%, endowment returns were strong. As I mentioned, there was a reduction in alt exposure, from 54% to 47% on average, for endowments. However, there is no indication that this tactical tweak means that alts are losing favor with endowments.[44]

However, although an option to enhancing diversification, the alternative space is unknown to many investors, and diversification does not assure a profit or protect against a loss in a declining market. Portfolios that have a greater percentage of alternatives may have great risks, especially those including arbitrage, currency, leveraging, and commodities. This additional risk can offset the benefit of diversification. As such, one consideration might be to purchase investment products that are managed by high-level experts with specialized skill sets that employ components of both fundamental and technical analysis, as well as risk management vehicles and procedures.

---

[43] James B. Stewart, *The Wall Street Journal*, "University Endowments Face a Hard Landing," October 2012.

[44] Tim Sturrock, *FundFire*, "Endowment Returns Strong, Alts Allocations Drop," November 7, 2013.

Radical Idea: Do Something Different

Previous generations utilized newspapers as their primary information source, yet the increased transparency and on-demand availability of information are two more components I think play a critical role in cyclical volatility. With new technological advances (cable news, Google™, financial blogs) facilitating the flow of information, investors now have the opportunity to react quickly to a given event, but not always in the most rational manner. This can, in turn, create even more volatility. As a result, the sheer volume of financial tools and information available today has greatly increased the speed with which high-volume trades can be executed. This is just one more catalyst for increasing volatility, and consequently, the increasing need for investors to do something different.

From the Alt Vault: Valuable Takeaways from Chapter Three

A new strategy is needed to help weather the highly volatile markets experienced in recent years. Alts may do this either by helping to reduce volatility in the individual portfolio or, where appropriate, attempting to use volatility as an advantage.

- Markets are increasingly cyclical.
- Too many investors missed the post-2008 rebound, unsure of how—or when—to get back in.
- The days of relying on buy-and-hold investing may be days gone by.
- Proper diversification is important in a strategic plan.
- With a smart strategy, investors (along with their financial professionals) can learn to use volatility to their advantage.

What's next: Globalization means markets are increasingly interconnected—and prone to volatility. A hiccup in a far-away land can cause major disruptions in the average investor's portfolio. If you think you're immune, think again. How can alternatives help?

Four
It's a Smaller World After All

Can a New Yorker get sick if someone sneezes in China?

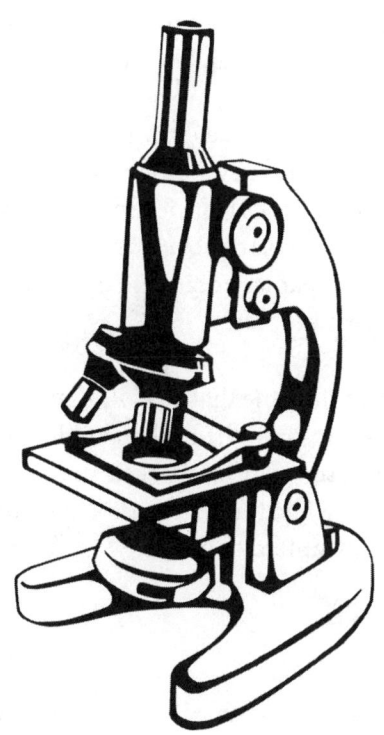

In our interconnected world, an epidemic can become a pandemic as the result of a simple sneeze.[45] Witness the panic surrounding the Severe Acute Respiratory Syndrome (SARS) epidemic of 2003. More than 700 of the 8,000 people who became infected died.[46] Even though actions by the Center for Disease Control likely prevented the disease from spreading to more parts of the world, global media perpetuated greater panic than was likely warranted. Concern over the disease disrupted international trade and travel, severely impacted tourism, and forced the cancellation of mass events. The Rolling Stones famously postponed a weekend set of stadium concerts in Hong Kong over fears of spreading the virus.

Such talk of contagions also applies to markets and investing. A ready metaphor involves the wave of bank failures and currency devaluations that swept across Asia just five years before the SARS outbreak. Aptly referred to as the Asian Flu, it began when Thailand, Indonesia, and South Korea fueled their country's economic growth with capital borrowed in U.S. dollars. These currencies soon fell dramatically in value when their link with the dollar proved unsustainable. As a result, the debt of many Asian companies became so expensive that their governments came close to bankruptcy.[47]

BBC News reported at the time that "...world markets are now so interlinked that a recession in one part of the world quickly affects trade in all regions. And because financial markets are even more closely tied together by global electronic trading, a crisis in confidence in one market will quickly be transmitted to others."[48]

---

[45] T. Déirdre Hollingsworth, Neil M. Ferguson, Roy M. Anderson, U.S. National Library of Medicine, "Frequent Travelers and Rate of Spread of Epidemics," September 2007.

[46] Center for Disease Control, "SARS—Basic Facts," July 2012.

[47] BBC News, "Catching the 'Asian Flu,'" June 1998.

[48] Ibid.

As the Asian financial crisis was unfolding, an American investment firm experienced a contagion threat of its own. On September 23, 1998, the Federal Reserve of New York reached an agreement with 14 financial banks to recapitalize Long-Term Capital Management, a Greenwich, Connecticut based hedge fund, in which the banks would provide the firm with emergency funds. The announcement capped a trying year for Long-Term Capital, which employed sophisticated strategies for high-net-worth investors and counted two Nobel Laureates, Myron Scholes and Robert Merton, as principals. In the late 1990s, the firm made investments in derivatives. They bet wrong, the markets turned, and the firm teetered on the edge of collapse. Because of the large amount of money involved and the co-mingling of global markets, the president of the Federal Reserve Bank of New York feared a global pandemic if the firm was to go under and therefore began recapitalization efforts with the help of European and domestic banks.[49] Of course, these events were just a hint of what was to come with other venerable Wall Street firms a decade later.

Booster Shot: Globalization Begins

This modern concept of globalization began with the Bretton Woods monetary system, named for the conference held by the Allied Nations in the New Hampshire wilderness in the waning days of the Second World War. It featured liberalization measures that set exchange rates between countries and oversaw creation of both the International Monetary Fund, as well as a precursor to what today is the World Bank.[50] This new era of global economic cooperation is one reason world trade has grown by an average of 6% per year, every year since World War II reconstruction began (with a few exceptions).[51]

---

[49] Roger Lowenstein, *New York Times*, "Long-Term Capital Management: It's a Short-term Memory," September 2008; Kimberly Amadeo, About.com, "What Was the Long-Term Capital Management Hedge Fund and the LTCM Crisis?" January 2012.

[50] The Levin Institute, The State University of New York, "International Monetary Fund and World Bank," 2013.

[51] World Trade Organization, "Growth, Jobs, Development, and Better International Relations, How Trade and the Multilateral Trading System Help," 2013.

One result of modern globalization is a corresponding acceleration of the wide availability of communication and information technology. This communication revolution has led to greater micro-level efficiencies. For instance, financial professionals can now instantly collect and evaluate data on everything from foreign markets to economic trends in other countries without having to travel overseas.

As this capability in communication has evolved, so has financial trading technology. For the first part of the 20th century, chalkboards, newspapers, and tickertape dominated financial communication. In 1960, the first Quotron system was developed, which employed magnetic tape and allowed brokers to retrieve stock prices from keyboards at their desks.[52] The introduction of personal computers in the 1980s ushered in an era of on-demand information and real-time quotes, something that continues to evolve with the Internet and now mobile devices.[53] I often say that one person with an iPad is probably more efficient than the output of an entire Wall Street office in the 1970s and 1980s. Tablet trading applications and online platforms provide real-time results, meaning that due to the increase in global dependency across time zones, trading never stops. However, it's a double-edged sword. Technology may build efficiencies through interconnections and integration, but it also builds interdependencies—making it easier for a contagion to spread.

For an illustration of how this interconnectedness increasingly fuels market growth and collapse, consider what happened with credit default swaps during the worldwide credit bubble of the last decade. Famously tagged as financial "weapons of mass destruction" [54] by legendary investor Warren Buffet, a credit default swap transfers the default risk from the security owner to swap seller.[55]

---

[52] Roy S. Freedman, Elsevier Inc., "Introduction to Financial Technology," 2006.

[53] Moss Strohem, *eHow*, "Software for Technical Analysis of Stocks," 2013.

[54] Cate Long, Reuters, "Column: Warren Buffett's Municipal Weapons of Mass Destruction," August 2012.

[55] Investopedia, "Credit Default Swap—CDS," 2013.

The underlying global credit default swap market size at the end of 2001 was $918 billion. By the end of 2007, investors had purchased swaps on underlying assets worth $62.3 trillion—a stratospheric 6,686% increase in just six years.[56] But eventually the housing bubble and credit crisis grew too big, *popped* in 2007, and started to wind down in 2009.[57] Credit default swaps are complex, and a detailed description of what they are and how they work could easily be the subject of another book entirely. Because they're so complex, the vast majority of retail investors would not hold swaps within their portfolio. But they provide a good illustration of how quickly bubbles can inflate and deflate, and how conditions in seemingly unrelated financial markets and countries across the globe can wreak havoc in the average investor's portfolio.

Immune System Breakdown: Volatility Reaches Fever Pitch

As a more recent example, on May 6, 2010, the Dow Jones Industrial Average lost almost 1,000 points in intraday trading in a period of 20 minutes, temporarily wiping out $1 trillion in market value.[58] What became known as the "flash crash" had never been seen before and was attributed to the activity of high-frequency traders and the rapid, electronic execution of trades.

If only this was an isolated incident. In August of 2012, the market experienced a "flash crash" when a software glitch caused the prices of 150 companies to suddenly spike. The hiccup occurred in the market-making unit of Knight Capital when a technical problem affected how trade orders were routed. The next day the company projected it would lose $440 million and within two days Knight Capital's stock value plummeted by 75%.[59] Barely a year later, in another incident, on

---

[56] Reuters, "How the Credit Default Swaps Market Works," October 15, 2008.

[57] Investopedia, "Market Crashes: Housing Bubble and Credit Crisis (2007–2009)," 2013.

[58] Reena Aggarwal, Center for Financial Markets and Policy, Georgetown University, "The Growth of Global ETFs and Regulatory Challenges," January 2012.

[59] Maureen Farrell, *CNN Money*, "Knight Capital Surges 60% as Trades Return," August, 2012.

August 22, 2013, trading on the NASDAQ, which includes companies such as Microsoft and Intel, shut down for three hours due to what officials at the exchange called a "technical glitch."[60]

The reality is that the investment world today is heavily dependent on information and the rapid flow of data. Technology is making our financial world smaller, and when someone sneezes, more and more people are likely to catch colds. Before 2008, many investors thought they were well diversified by holding international stocks, emerging markets, high-yield bonds, and real estate in addition to more traditional equities. However, over time, correlation rose between these types of investments and the S&P 500, and investors were not as well diversified as they were before. The overall rise in correlation of traditional investments, something that made the 2008 economic crisis devastating to so many investors, can now quickly spread throughout the globe.

So why then would an investor even want to invest internationally?

Modern Medicine: Combating Home Country Bias

If one studies the allocation of the average investor, their assets are overwhelmingly located within the country they reside. To put it plainly, Americans buy American stocks. Known as "home country bias," American investors had over 70% of their equity investments in U.S. domestic stocks as of 2012.[61] While growth in emerging and developing

---

[60] *Washington Post*, "Nasdaq Resumes Trading After Technical Glitch," August 22, 2013.

[61] International Monetary Fund's Coordinated Portfolio Investment Survey (2012); International Monetary Fund's Coordinated Direct Investment Survey (2012). MSCI Data as of 12/31/2012. Notes: The IMF's Coordinated Portfolio Investment Survey and Coordinated Direct Investment Survey were used in conjunction with market-cap information to determine domestic and foreign investment. The MSCI USA (IMI) was used to represent the United States equity market portfolio.

economies has recently slowed, they are still predicted to grow at a rate of 5.1% in 2014, compared to a growth of 2.0% in advanced economies, and 3.6% for the world overall.[62] With the wide availability of domestic asset management companies (mutual fund and ETF managers, for instance) that offer international investment opportunities in various regions of the world, the practice of home country bias may be unsound. Just as it makes little sense to concentrate a portfolio in one company's stock, it makes little sense to concentrate a portfolio in one industry, sector, and yes, country. Of course, international investing does not come without risks, such as exposure to potentially adverse local political and economic developments; nationalization and exchange controls; potentially lower liquidity and higher volatility; possible problems arising from accounting, disclosure, settlement, and regulatory practices that differ from U.S. standards; and the chance that fluctuations in foreign rates will decrease the investment's value.

Even with all of the above, international allocations can still act as a further diversification[63] tool. A truly global investor learns to recognize there are segments within the global marketplace that are priced attractively at any given time. As such, they are not concerned about pulling back to American shores simply due to one crisis in one particular area of the world. A well-thought-out investment strategy takes into consideration opportunity at every point within an economic cycle and recognizes the importance of seeking opportunity globally in addition to the investor's geographic base.

To put it more plainly, although globalization led to an increased risk of "catching a cold," secluding oneself at home may not be the cure, especially if you live with others that act as carriers.

---

[62] Rupa Duttagupta and Thomas Helbing, International Monetary Fund, "World Economic Outlook: Global Growth, Patterns Shifting, Says IMF WEO," October 8, 2013.

[63] Diversification does not assure a profit or protect against loss in a declining market.

Second Opinion: The Best Advisors Seek the Counsel of Their Peers

A global investment strategy calls for a measured approach, one that is executed with the help of one, or a number, of investment professionals. The investing climate has become so crowded with different strategies and opportunities that, increasingly, even investment professionals are seeking the counsel of their peers in finding hidden potential. According to the old adage, "even the doctor needs to see a doctor," and we all know that someone who represents themselves in a legal matter "has a fool for a client." Consequently, financial and investment opportunities may exist where one may not have thought and may be uncovered with the help of those with a particular expertise in one sector or geographic area of the globe.

For instance, some emerging market countries were not as affected by the global financial meltdown of 2008 and had better fiscal balance sheets with their government debt than many developed nations.[64] In fact, as evident from Figure 4.1, while the average GDP for emerging market and developing economies fell in 2008, it remained positive at 2.7 compared to negative GDP in advanced economies at -3.5. As a result, when the dust settled, investors realized emerging markets had differing growth rates.[65] Yet the news comes fast and often; by mid-2013, emerging markets were back on their heels, hit hard by rising inflation, sliding currencies in many others, and a slowdown in Chinese economic growth.[66]

Many markets in the developed world were just as volatile, yet despite the barrage of headlines in recent years, not all countries in Europe are the hopeless cases the press would have you believe. In fact, in 2012, European banks restructured and, in some cases, were forced to

---

[64] Maureen Nevin Duffy, Oxstone Investment Club, "ETFs Provide Exposure to Emerging Markets Growth and Risk," April 2012.

[65] Thomas Kenny, About.com, "Investing in Emerging Market Corporate Bonds: The Next Frontier," 2013.

[66] Tom Lydon, ETFTrends.com, "Emerging Markets 'Triple Threat' Could Hurt These ETFs," August 21, 2013.

deleverage by selling distressed assets at reduced prices[67] (similar to what happened with U.S. banks in 2008). Sophisticated investors and money managers took advantage of these deleveraging requirements by making strategic trades in those distressed assets. As an example, a number of hedge funds bought new, distressed asset offerings from the banking sector,[68] believing their quick infusions of capital would be rewarded.

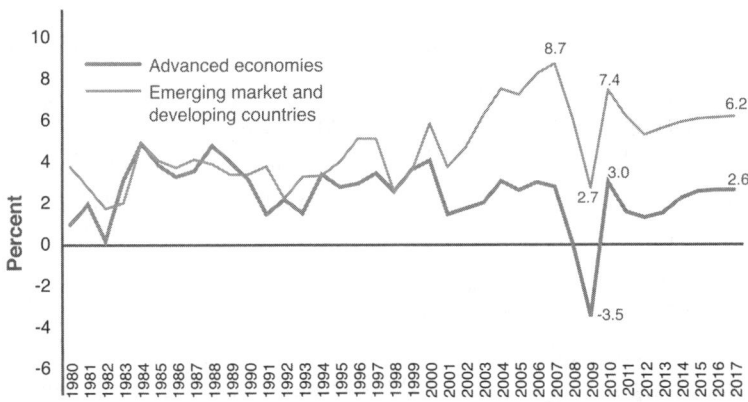

Figure 4.1

Beyond Europe, many other countries appeared (and are still appearing) in global investment discussions. The Brazilian bond market that was once hot quickly cooled.[69] Middle Eastern markets looked attractive in 2012 relative to their past performance.[70]

---

[67] Anne-Sylvaine Chassany, Bloomberg, "Europe Banks Fail to Cut as Draghi Loans Defer Deleverage," September 2012.

[68] Bob Parker, Seeking Alpha, "Bank Deleveraging, Opportunities Expected But No Gold Rush," August 2012.

[69] Rob Dwyer, Euromoney, "Debt Capital Markets: Brazil DCM is No Longer a Darling Abroad," October 2012.

[70] Rabah Arezki and Mustapha K. Nabli, IMF Working Paper, "Natural Resources, Volatility, and Inclusive Growth: Perspectives from the Middle East and North Africa," April 2012.

Fatal Mistake: Do Nothing

Regardless of how investors feel about the issue of globalization, access to money managers with specialized investment expertise in sectors and geographic locations are now available, but most individuals have yet to take advantage. A "do-it-yourselfer" faces the task of gathering and understanding all of the information available to appropriately manage such a wide array of potential options. It was a difficult task with traditional, long-only investments—even more so now with the advent of non-correlated and counter-correlated investments.

For example, if someone was looking to invest in real estate in China, they could probably find someone in New York to help. But wouldn't it be better to partner with someone on the ground, who knows the culture, people, and politics of the world's largest developing market? These "partners" are now increasingly available to the average retail investor.

It's tempting to throw up your hands in surrender and bury your head, but to do nothing can be harmful. The increasingly longer life spans discussed in the first chapter, and the issues they bring, mean investors who sit it out are sitting still. Investment professionals are available to help, but one must be prudent in their choice of whom to hire. How is this done? How does one go about allocating money and assets across investments? Questions we will now discuss.

From the Alt Vault: Valuable Takeaways from Chapter Four

Is the cure worse than the cold? Globalization has brought the world closer together, and investing in once-overlooked, far-off lands may help provide sought after diversification. However, faster communication means quicker real-time adjustments, and often more volatility. The key is acting on the former while managing the latter. Experienced financial professionals can help.

- Our globalized, hyper-connected world can affect the investor's portfolio.
- Advances in technology and increased availability of on-demand information may have contributed to the correlation of traditional investments—investors can now make instant adjustments to their portfolio in response to breaking news from around the globe.
- Diversification is often hampered by "home country bias" or investing in what we know.
- If your portfolio has problems, doing nothing won't solve them.

What's next: Too often, investors have no one but themselves to blame. Bad behavior and a lack of proper investment "nutrition" conspire with global factors to negatively affect portfolio health. How can these bad behaviors be identified and overcome?

Five
Disappearing Diversification

What can investors learn from a lemonade stand?

Think back to that summer lemonade stand you operated as a kid. On hot sunny days you couldn't keep up with demand from neighborhood children, parents' yard work, or teenagers developing their tans. But what about the long winter days when everyone was trapped inside? Were you forced to wait out weeks or months of the season with no profits? Success was largely dependent on the uncontrollable variables of temperature and the climate in which you operated. If you only offered lemonade, you probably only made money on sunny days.

But what if you offered an alternative, one suited to the changing seasons? Perhaps you opened a hot chocolate stand where everyone was sledding? By branching out with diverse offerings, you had the potential to earn a profit year round, regardless of the weather.

Individuals can't control the weather any more than investors can control globalization, regulations, unexpected events, new innovations, or human behavior. And since we can't change market inputs, maybe it's time we changed the way we invest (remember that investing has inherent risks, and a change in strategy will not guarantee better results).

If we're going to change our strategies, we need to understand why we make the financial choices we do. This is the question proponents of behavioral finance, including Princeton professor and Nobel Laureate Daniel Kahneman, have been trying to answer for decades. In 1979, Kahneman wrote a widely regarded paper with Amos Tversky on the subject of behavioral economics that introduced the phrase "prospect theory."[71] "If you want an easy introduction to behavioral economics, it's economics without making the assumption that [investors] are fully rational or that they have perfect self-control," Kahneman told *AdvisorOne* in late 2011.[72] Specifically, behavioral finance identifies the psychological reasons investors make decisions, reasons of which they are often unaware.

---

[71] Floris Heukelom, Amsterdam School of Economics, "Kahneman and Tversky and the Origin of Behavioral Economics," May 2006.

[72] John Sullivan, *AdvisorOne*, "Behavioral Economics: Your Own Worst Enemy," January 2012.

Sugary Sweet: Learning Self-Control

Kahneman's work identifies two primary investor traits that inadvertently harm long-term portfolio performance: hope for gain and fear of loss,[73] known as the aforementioned prospect theory. It's the idea that fear originates not only in our desire to avoid investment loss, but also, to a lesser extent, to avoid missing out on potential gain. I believe the now legendary collapse of energy firm Enron at the beginning of the last decade is an excellent example of prospect theory.

Throughout the bull market of the 1980s and 1990s, many companies saw their stock prices skyrocket. This may have caused employees to overinvest in their companies' stock plans, thinking the stock would continue to rise into perpetuity, or perhaps they believed that since they worked at that particular company, they would recognize signs of potential danger and divest in time. Personally, I think it was the influence of fear and greed.

Consider the bankruptcy of Enron. Employees were more focused on their portfolio statements than the shoddy theories fueling their returns. This was demonstrated by an extremely high adoption rate among its staff in the stock ownership plan offered by the company, with some employees investing 100% of their retirement funds. Even when troubles began to emerge, many held on to stock, afraid to miss out on potential gains.[74] For that reason, diversification didn't seem to matter.

As the company imploded, management eventually instituted a "temporary freeze," preventing employees from selling their stock in an effort to slow the descent. By the time the freeze was lifted, the company was on the verge of collapse and the stock was virtually worthless.[75]

---

[73] Investopedia, "Prospect Theory," 2013.

[74] Christine Dugas, *USA Today*, "Energy Giant's Disaster Devastates 401(k) Plans," November 2001.

[75] Christine Dugas, *USA Today*, "Employees' Faith in Enron Cost Them Life Savings," January 2002.

Of course the public outcry at the financial malfeasance of Enron CEOs was intense and widespread. At the same time, I would say that former Enron employees became the poster children for the dangers of not employing a diversified plan.

You hope investors would learn, but how many tragic tales were aired in the wake of the Ponzi scheme perpetrated by Bernie Madoff, in which retires lost their homes, moved in with their children, or were forced back to work?

But diversification is more than simply investing in different companies. Investors seeking to diversify their portfolio also must look at how connected, or correlated, their investments are. Today there is a myriad of investment options and vehicles used to lower correlation in a portfolio. While diversification and lack of correlation do not necessarily remove risk and losses can still be incurred, diversification is an important investment strategy. But with so many options, how does an investor know the right way to go?

Similar Taste: The Rise of Correlation

Probably the greatest consideration for including alternative investments in a portfolio is the rise in correlation in recent years. As I briefly discussed in earlier chapters, the term *correlation*, as it refers to stock market performance, asset classes, or sectors, is a measure of how likely they are to move in either the same or opposite direction. If they are positively correlated, they will move in lock step with one another, either by rising or falling together, which is precisely the problem. When one falls, the other is likely to follow.

Correlation is a market-driven outcome that directly affects the benefits of diversification. Higher correlations are an indication of lower diversification. For example, you can see by the matrix in Figure 5.1 that U.S. equity, as measured by the Russell 3000, and international equity, as measured by the MSCI EAFE (an index that measures equity performance in developed markets outside the United States and Canada), have a high correlation of 0.90.[76]

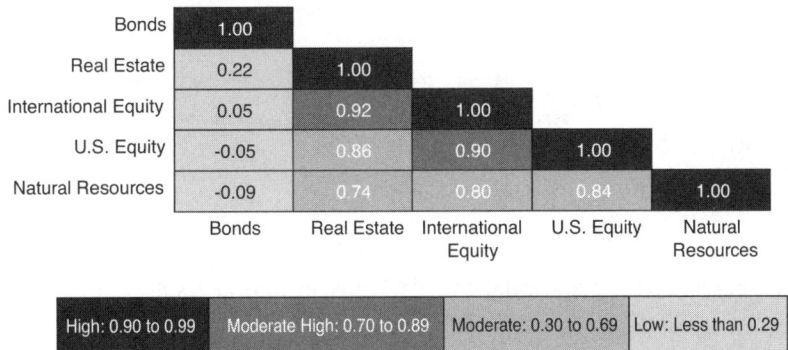

Figure 5.1

Zooming into the correlation between U.S. and international equity, in 10-year increments, over the last 30 years (ended 12/31/2013) we've also seen the correlation between U.S. and international stocks almost double, from 0.43 to 0.89,[77] as can be seen in Figure 5.2.

---

[76] Lipper, a Thomson Reuters Company, January 2014.
[77] Ibid.

Chapter Five Disappearing Diversification

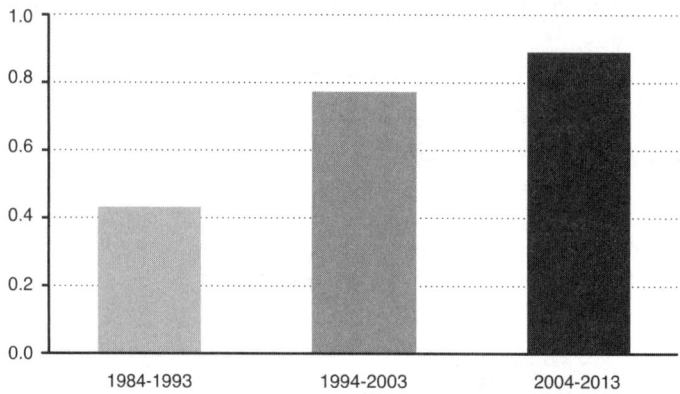

Figure 5.2

The increase in international correlation is partially a result of the reduction of trade barriers and improved political environments that came about after the end of the Cold War. In the same way global economies are becoming more interconnected, multinational corporations are also increasingly dependent on international sales. For example, Coca-Cola® (which is based in Atlanta) is "...one of the most globally active international companies, derived 80 percent of its sales from outside the U.S."[78] Conversely, Samsung®, a Korean-based company, had 47 percent of its sales in America in 2011.[79]

---

[78] William J. Holstein, Strategy+Business, "How Coca-Cola Manages 90 Emerging Markets," November 2011.

[79] Samsung Electronics, "Sustainability Report," 2012.

According to Morningstar© 2014 Morningstar, Inc.,* this rise in correlation isn't confined to individual stocks. Companies in the same industries that together comprise many of the S&P 500 sectors have also become more highly correlated within the S&P 500 Index. Between 1994 and 2008, 69% of the average monthly returns of the investment sectors included in the index were correlated, meaning they moved in tandem. In the four years since, that number has increased to 84%. Morningstar notes that no decline in correlation was seen in any of the S&P 500 Index's 10 sectors. Even utilities, the least correlated sector, rose from 38% to 67%. More concerning, correlation between large-cap and small-cap stocks in 2012 was at its highest level in 60 years.[80]

Investors may think they are properly diversified by investing in different companies, sectors, and even countries around the globe, and honestly, who could blame them? The distressing fact is, increasingly they are not, something of which they are too often unaware. Yet as correlation decreases, so too does the possibility of its corresponding risk in the portfolio. Alternative investments are not only *moderately to lowly* correlated to traditional stocks and bonds, they're also not very correlated with each other (as the "Correlations Across Various Investments" chart in Figure 5.3 illustrates).

---

* All Rights Reserved. The information contained herein: (1) is proprietary to Morningstar and/or its content providers; (2) may not be copied or distributed; (3) does not constitute investment advice offered by Morningstar; and (4) is not warranted to be accurate, complete or timely. Neither Morningstar nor its content providers are responsible for any damages or losses arising from any use of this information. Past performance is no guarantee of future results. Use of information from Morningstar does not necessarily constitute agreement by Morningstar, Inc. of any investment philosophy or strategy presented in this publication

[80] Michael Rawson, Morningstar, "The Correlation Conundrum and What to Do About It," May 9, 2012.

Correlation Across Various Investments
2008–2013

	Bonds	Covered Calls	Convertible Arbitrage	Merger Arbitrage	Managed Futures	Global Infrastructure	Commodities	Real Estate	Gold Equity	Emerging Market Debt	International Equity	Emerging Mkt. Equity	U.S. Equity	Private Equity	Natural Resources
Bonds	1.00														
Covered Calls	0.02	1.00													
Convertible Arbitrage	-0.03	0.38	1.00												
Merger Arbitrage	-0.07	0.58	0.52	1.00											
Managed Futures	0.34	0.10	0.09	0.15	1.00										
Global Infrastructure	0.20	0.77	0.42	0.60	0.31	1.00									
Commodities	0.01	0.61	0.39	0.56	0.28	0.66	1.00								
Real Estate	0.22	0.76	0.46	0.56	0.18	0.85	0.63	1.00							
Gold Equity	0.22	0.22	0.22	0.29	0.29	0.25	0.56	0.19	1.00						
Emerging Market Debt	0.50	0.50	0.45	0.50	0.22	0.71	0.49	0.72	0.31	1.00					
International Equity	0.05	0.78	0.49	0.73	0.19	0.86	0.69	0.92	0.22	0.64	1.00				
Emerging Mkt. Equity	0.11	0.73	0.53	0.72	0.13	0.77	0.72	0.86	0.40	0.73	0.88	1.00			
U.S. Equity	-0.05	0.89	0.40	0.64	0.13	0.79	0.64	0.86	0.22	0.50	0.90	0.82	1.00		
Private Equity	0.08	0.77	0.45	0.62	0.07	0.76	0.58	0.91	0.20	0.58	0.90	0.85	0.91	1.00	
Natural Resources	-0.09	0.77	0.50	0.63	0.14	0.70	0.82	0.74	0.53	0.51	0.80	0.83	0.84	0.77	1.00

High: 0.90 to 0.99 | Moderate High: 0.70 to 0.89 | Moderate: 0.30 to 0.69 | Low: 0.00 to 0.29 | Negative: Less than 0.00

Chart created by Jackson National Life Insurance Company (Home office: Lansing, Michigan) utilizing data from Lipper, a Thomson Reuters Company. Each asset class is represented by an index. The index definitions can be found in the glossary. Bonds=Barclays U.S. Aggregate Bond index, Covered Calls=CBOE S&P 500 Buywrite index, Covertible Arbitrage= Credit Suisse Cnvrt Arb Hedge Fund index, Merger Arbitrage=Credit Suisse ED Rsk Arb Hedge Fund, Managed Futures=Credit Suisse Mngd Fut Hedge Fund, Global Infrastructre=Dow Jones Brookfield Global Infrastructure index, Commodities=Dow Jones-UBS Commodity index, Real Estate = FTSE EPRA/NAREIT Developed index, Gold Equity=FTSE Gold Mines index, Emerging Market Debt=JP Morgan EMBI Global Diversified index, International Equity=MSCI EAFE index, Emerging Market Equity=MSCI EM (Emerging Markets) index, U.S. Equity=Russell 3000 index, Private Equity=S&P Listed Private Equity index, Natural Resources=S&P North American Natural Resources Sector index.

Figure 5.3

Proper Diversification: A Well-Balanced Diet

Asset allocation and proper diversification mean different things to different people, but the important lesson is to not concentrate your portfolio in any one vehicle or investment type. Think of it in terms of a balanced diet. What constitutes "balanced" will depend on a person's age, height, weight, medical situation, allergies, and other characteristics specific to the individual. But one thing is certain: a diet that *only* consisted of breads and cereals would not be considered healthy. And so it is with a person's investment portfolio—the individual's allocation of assets will depend on age, goals, years to retirement, and other factors.

In my opinion, the need for proper diversification within the portfolio will only continue to increase, and it is happening at exactly the same time our "interconnected world" is making it that much harder for the everyday investor to achieve due to increasing correlation.

Thirst for Diversification: Develop an All-Weather Strategy

What this means is that an international and domestic strategy for sunny and rainy days, in good markets and bad, plays a big role in investor success. I feel strongly that alternative investments can play a significant role in that strategy. By helping to provide further diversification due to their historically low correlation to traditional investments, they can help the portfolio by moving independently of stocks, bonds, and each other, through changing climates.

The accompanying graph in Figure 5.4 illustrates how making a minor tweak in a portfolio by adding alternative investments increased returns and lowered risk. Past performance is no guarantee of future results. As you can see, when the allocation to alternatives in the portfolio increased, average annual returns went up and annual standard deviation (also known as risk) went down.

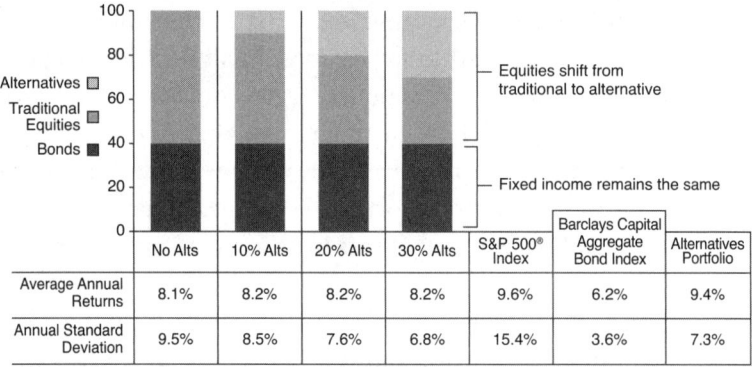

Figure 5.4

Although asset allocation among different asset categories generally limits exposure to any one category, the risk remains that an asset category that performs poorly relative to the other asset categories may be favored. Other investment risks include general economic risk, geopolitical risk, commodity-price volatility, counterparty and settlement risk, currency risk, derivatives risk, emerging markets risk, foreign securities risk, high-yield bond exposure, noninvestment-grade bond exposure, index investing risk, industry concentration risk, leveraging risk, market risk, prepayment risk, liquidity risk, real estate investment risk, sector risk, short sales risk, temporary defensive positions, and large cash positions. Diversification does not assure a profit or protect against loss in a declining market. Past performance is no guarantee of future results. Alternatives may also negate the benefits of diversification.

From the Alt Vault: Valuable Takeaways from Chapter Five

The important lesson is not to concentrate the portfolio in any one vehicle or investment type. Just like the best lemonade is a combination of several key ingredients, a well-balanced portfolio may incorporate many different opportunities. Alternatives are one way investors can diversify their portfolio.

- Markets cannot be controlled, however, investors can control their reaction to them.
- Fear and greed can lead to poor judgment.
- Individual stocks and markets are becoming increasingly correlated.
- In our interconnected world, portfolios need balance.
- Develop a strategy for sunny and rainy days; consider one that includes alternative investments to help manage the volatility.

What's next: How do institutional investors build their portfolios? Where do they get their ideas? Where are their sights set now?

Six
Exploring the Alternative Universe

Where does the rubber meet the road?

Goodyear Tire and Rubber Co. is best known for its brand of tires (as well as the dirigible blimp that bears its name). However, the company undertakes research and development in lesser known, but I think equally important, areas that intersect business and science. In 1971, Goodyear worked with NASA to develop a new tire that could withstand the treacherous conditions on Mars. The result was a new material that was stronger than steel. Recognizing the increased durability of the material, Goodyear engineers introduced the technology in its consumer-based business and went on to produce a new radial tire with a tread life expected to be 16,000 kilometers (approximately 10,000 miles) longer than conventional radial tires.[81] More recently Goodyear again partnered with NASA to develop an energy efficient, airless "Spring Tire" for further exploration both in space and on Earth.[82]

Flight Plan: Collaborate to Win

NASA was involved in the design and development of something that Goodyear eventually marketed to consumers. Likewise, I've observed that many financial services companies have taken the portfolio model designs developed by institutional investors and used them to create similar products for their retail investors. Investment banks, brokerage firms, mutual fund companies, insurance companies, endowment funds, pension funds, and hedge funds are all examples of institutional investors.

---

[81] Peter Nowak, *MSN Tech & Gadgets*, "10 Surprising NASA Inventions: Stronger Tires," 2013.

[82] AutoBlog, "Goodyear 'Spring Tire' Engineered to Withstand the Harshest Environments on the Moon and Possibly the Toughest Places on Earth," March 2012.

For example, David Swensen, chief investment officer at Yale University, is famous in the investment world for his exploration of new strategies. It's no simple task, but one that I would assume has been key to the well-being of the funds he's charged with overseeing. After all, he is responsible for managing and investing Yale's endowment, worth more than $18 billion as of October 2012.[83]

In Figure 6.1, "Swenson's Sweet Spot: 10-Year Returns," you see Swensen's historical average annual return was 11.8% over the 10-year period from 1999 to 2009 on his investments.[84] This historical period is significant because it encompasses a major portion of the economic downturn in 2008. During the same time, the broader S&P 500 Index returned less than 1%.[85] Swensen's consistent track record has the attention of top Wall Street money managers, all wondering how he does it. His consistency is one reason he's held his position with Yale for almost three decades.[86]

Swensen applies a variation of Modern Portfolio Theory (discussed in Chapter One) which attempts to increase returns for any given level of risk. He revised this theory in his groundbreaking book, *Pioneering Portfolio Management*.

---

[83] Yale University, About Yale, "Chief Investment Officer David Frederick Swensen," 2012.

[84] Seeking Alpha, "Top Investor Swensen Has High Conviction in These 3 Companies," March 22, 2012.

[85] Lipper, a Thomson Reuters Company, May 2013.

[86] Seeking Alpha, "Top Investor Swensen Has High Conviction in These 3 Companies," March 22, 2012.

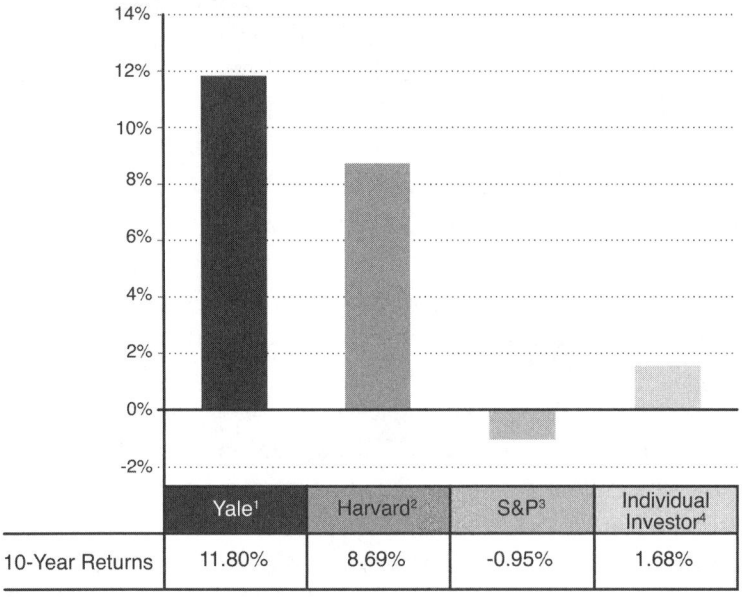

Figure 6.1

Swensen developed this variation with Dean Takahashi. The method, once given the nickname "The Yale Model," is now commonly known as "The Endowment Model" as many other funds have attempted to replicate Swensen's success. This model is characterized by heavy allocations to different asset classes when compared with conventional portfolios. It consists broadly of dividing a portfolio into seven or eight parts and dividing the money amongst different investment categories, which roll up to five asset classes.[87]

---

[87] Yale University, "2012: The Yale Endowment," 2012.

As shown in the "Swensen's Asset Allocations" chart in Figure 6.2, the Yale Portfolio generally has smaller allocations to asset classes with low expected returns such as fixed income and money markets, in favor of non-correlated assets. Non-correlated assets could be investments such as private equity and other alternative investments.

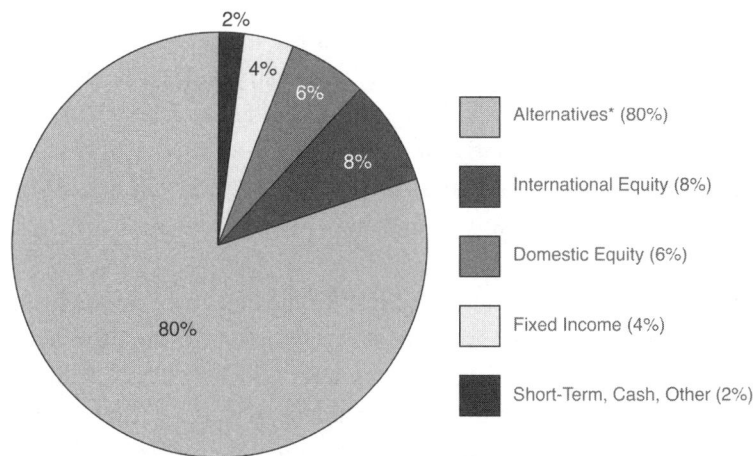

Chart created by Jackson National Life Insurance Company (Home office: Lansing, Michigan) utilizing data from "2012: The Yale Endowment," Yale University.
*Alternatives include absolute return, natural resources, private equity, and real estate.

Figure 6.2

Investing can be considered both an art and a science. As we've learned from the field of behavioral finance, many investors still cling to outdated prejudices, emotional responses, and superstitions not suited to successful strategies in the modern portfolio. I see the art of investing as adjusting and interpreting according to what investors anticipate will happen in the future. The science is based on math and a revised Modern Portfolio Theory. Revising MPT and updating it to reflect non-correlated inputs and variations likely not present at the time the original theory was developed is, in my opinion, much more desirable than rejecting it outright.

Down to Earth: What It Means for the Average Investor

As we saw in our Goodyear example, technology innovation driven by very smart people can eventually benefit the average consumer. This technology is now causing the financial industry to experience significant change. Or is it really a change at all? Some think alternatives are just a trend. I think alternative investments are a movement driven by the institutional market's search for better risk-adjusted returns and increasing need for diversification.[88]

Analysis by Eager, Davis, and Holmes found that from the beginning of 2011 to late 2012, investors added more money to alternative investments than to equity and fixed income combined—$94.6 billion in alternative investments (real estate included), versus a combined $79.6 billion to equities and fixed income that same year.

Consider that only $15.4 billion was committed to alternative investments and real estate *just eight years earlier* in 2003 by North American institutional investors. In that same year, investors made $65.9 billion of combined investments in equities and fixed income (excluding balanced and global tactical asset allocation mandates).[89] What does this mean? As markets in this country and around the world have expanded, alternative strategies are receiving a disproportionate share of these assets.

If the increasing speed with which alternatives are being adopted by institutional investors is any indication, I would say the trend towards

---

[88] Virginia Munger Kahn, *Financial Advisor*, "Alternatives Becoming Mainstream," July 2012.

[89] Tracker Hiring Analytics, Database of Institutional Investment Manager Hires, Eager, Davis, and Holmes.

alternatives is unlikely to end any time soon. After reaffirming that the "60% equities/40% fixed-income allocation that was standard decades ago is long gone," Mr. Kloepfer told *Pension & Investments* that "the typical public pension plan's fixed-income allocation, for example, could start heading toward 20%," and "many plans already are in the 20% to 30% range for fixed income."[90] Much of it is fueled by the "danger in safety" that exists in bonds.

Rising interest rates expose investors to interest rate risk; low yield that has plagued the space in recent years now means investors are paying a premium to own bonds. This is a premium they're unlikely to recover anytime soon due to the end of historically low interest rates imposed by the Federal Reserve's quantitative easing policy. The volatility introduced by the end of the policy was acutely felt in the summer of 2013, when talk of a program commonly referred to as "tapering" by the Fed led to $61.7 billion in bond mutual fund and ETF redemptions in June of that year, which was a record amount. As *ThinkAdvisor.com* noted at the time, the outflow "far exceeds the previous record monthly outflow of $41.8 billion at the height of the financial crisis in October 2008."[91]

So, where is that money going now? It may be going to alternative investments.

In addition to *Pension & Investments* and Callan's findings, research firm Morningstar, along with Barron's, reported that at the beginning of 2012, approximately 65% of financial advisors and 67% of institutions surveyed said that alternative investments "...are as important as or more important than traditional investments, down slightly from the last survey."[92] The survey included 264 institutional investors and 365 advisors.

---

[90] Arleen Jacobius, *Pensions & Investments*, "Institutional Investors Quicken Shift to Alternative Investments," September 2012.

[91] John Sullivan, "Bond Mutual Funds, ETFs Post Record Outflow," *ThinkAdvisor.com*, June 28, 2013.

[92] Morningstar, "Annual Survey Finds Continued Strong Usage of Alternative Investments Among Institutions and Financial Advisors But Growth Slowing," May 29, 2012.

Similarly, Russell Investments' *2012 Global Survey on Alternative Investing* found that institutions participating in the survey have made "significant allocations to alternatives"—on average 22% of total fund assets. The majority of respondents expect to keep their alternative allocations the same or increase them in the next one to three years, with expected increases to alternatives such as hedge funds and private real estate.[93] The survey included 144 organizations totaling $1.1 trillion in assets.

Institutional managers such as David Swensen have found success in the alternative investments market, which brought attention to these strategies from retail investors. Most likely the increasing correlation (discussed in Chapter Four) and disappearing diversification associated with traditional investments are driving sophisticated institutional investors to alternative investments as well.

Alternative Investments: No Longer So Alien

What it all means is that interest in alternative investments may be growing. Historically, many financial innovations were once likely considered alternative. Although Massachusetts Investors Trust, largely thought of as the first contemporary mutual fund, was created and deployed in the 1920s, it wasn't until the bull market in the 1980s that mutual funds gained widespread adoption and acceptance.[94] Today mutual funds are a common addition to portfolios and currently hold trillions of investable dollars. The chart in Figure 6.3 measures the growth of mutual funds, as well as their assets, since 1940.

---

[93] Russell Investments, "Russell 2012 Global Survey on Alternative Investing Finds Institutional Investors Looking to Alternatives for Both Diversification and Alpha," June 2012.

[94] James E. McWhinney, Investopedia, "A Brief History of the Mutual Fund," September 7, 2009.

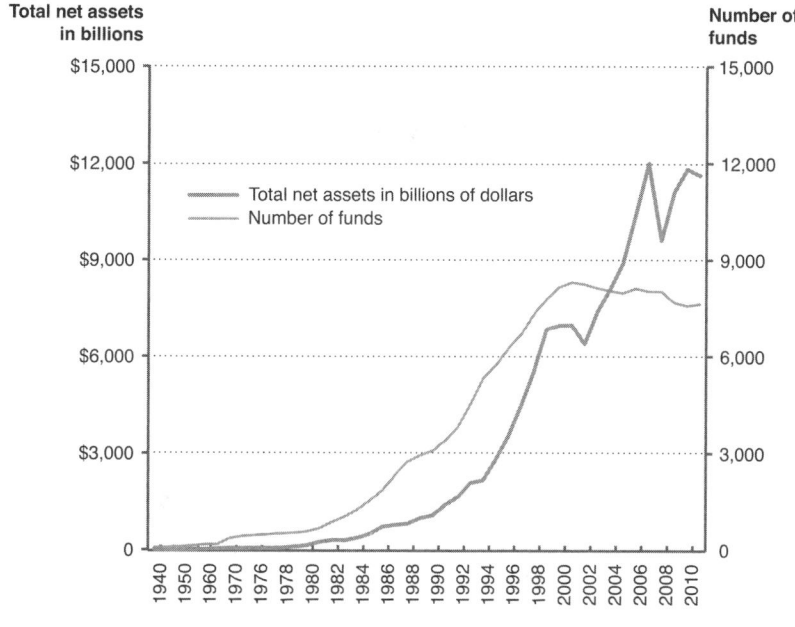

Figure 6.3

More recently (and as discussed in the Chapter Three), an increase in wealth and average standard of living in many emerging market countries is a direct result of globalization that began post-World War II. Through the advent of emerging market mutual funds and similar products, countries once considered exotic and far-flung, now offer many investing opportunities. In fact, the GDP growth of developing countries has outpaced that of developed since the global economic crisis of 2008.[95] Who would have thought, even as recently as a few years ago, that South Africa, Laos, Vietnam, and many other so-called frontier markets would offer the potential that they have recently—so much so that many mutual fund companies now offer investment strategies that

---

[95] The World Bank, "GDP Growth (Annual Percent)," 2013.

provide exposure to these regions?[96] As you look at Figure 6.4, observe how the GDP growth of developing countries has outpaced that of the U.S.

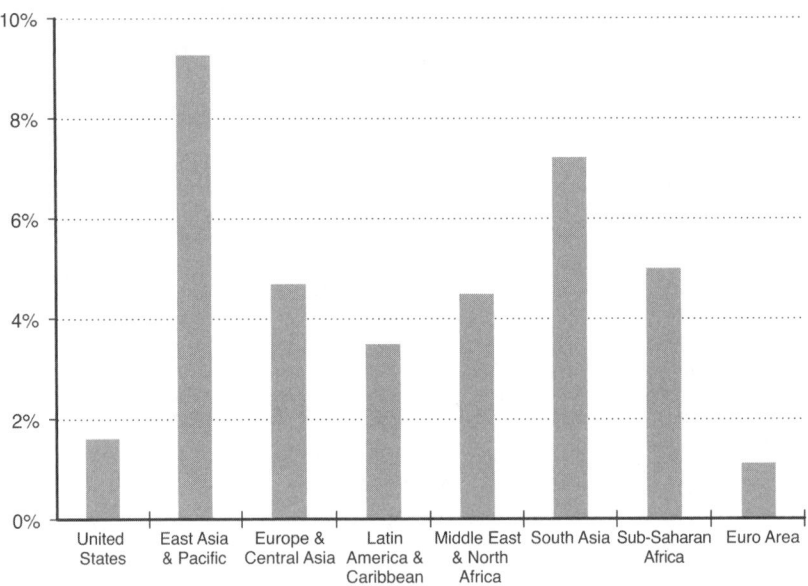

Figure 6.4

Yet recent headlines haven't made it easy to take advantage of these offerings. Scandals involving once-trusted financial titans have left some individuals understandably skeptical of anything new or perceived as untested.

---

[96] Conrad De Aenlle, *New York Times*, "Looking to Frontier Markets for the Next Big Thing in Investing," April 2012.

I've seen that too few realize that alternative investments aren't new and in many cases have a long track record in the institutional markets. However, alternatives just recently gained the attention of Main Street investors, thanks in large part to the success of strategies employed by endowment and other institutional investors, and their recent collaborations with financial services companies. Over the last six years, 1,012 alternative products have been introduced, in the form of public securities (mutual funds, ETFs, ETNs, and closed-end funds). Their popularity should continue to grow as asset managers have plans to create more alternative investment products than traditional investment products over the next 12 months. In fact, these same managers anticipate that, on average, alternative mutual fund assets will comprise 13.6% of total assets by the end of 2023.[97]

From the Alt Vault: Valuable Takeaways from Chapter Six

Although new ideas are often met with skepticism, good ideas are able to stick around and gain public approval. Just as important technology often starts with NASA engineers, important alternative investment concepts have been ignited by institutional investors—and mainstream investors are starting to take notice.

- Collaborative efforts can lead to cutting edge products and strategies, but not all ideas make smart investments.
- Investors should start thinking beyond the two-dimensional world of stocks and bonds.
- Investing is both art and science.
- Investors can't be the Magellan of their portfolios without a little exploring.
- Money is moving towards alternatives as part of some investors' diversification strategy.

---

[97] Cerulli Associates, *The Cerulli Report*, "Alternative Products and Strategies," pages 68, 72, 76, 2013.

What's next: The improper understanding of risk results in the slow erosion of assets and purchasing power over time. What's to be done? It might be as simple as a few more swings at bat.

Seven
Play the Percentages

How do you improve your batting average?

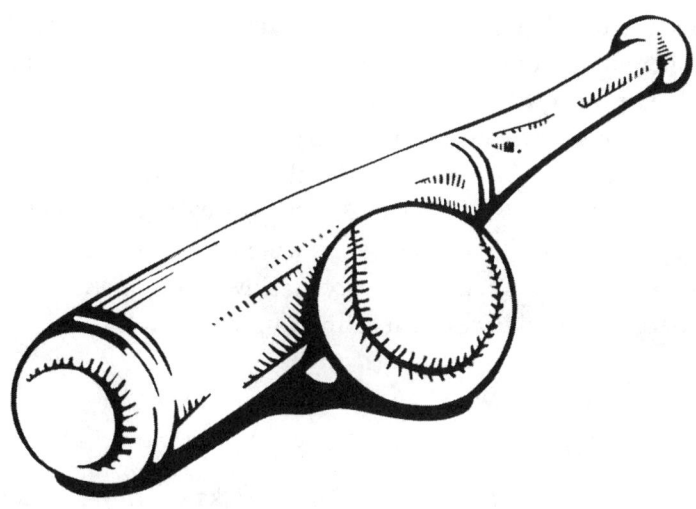

Consider the following quote from Kevin Costner's character Crash Davis, a perennial minor league baseball player from the 1988 movie *Bull Durham*, as he describes the risk/reward of the percentage hitter.

> "Know what the difference is between hitting .250 and hitting .300 is? It's 25 hits. Twenty-five hits in 500 at bats is 50 points, okay? There's six months in a season, that's about 25 weeks. That means if you get just one extra flare a week—just one—a gorp...a ground ball with eyes... a dying quail—just one more dying quail a week... and you're in Yankee Stadium!"[98]

When some people imagine risk they think of a one-time event that offers incredible gains or devastating losses. Not understanding risk and taking proper action can result in the slow erosion of assets and purchasing power over an extended period of time. It is only when the investor is preparing for retirement that the leak is discovered. A perfect example is inflation risk—the risk that the price of general goods and services will rise over time, thereby reducing present-value purchasing power. Because inflation generally occurs slowly, it is often overlooked by investors, who fail to realize its impact until it's too late.

Risk Mitigation: Eye on the Ball

Further explaining Costner's rant, ignore walks, sacrifices, and extra base hits. A baseball player with approximately four at-bats per game may have close to 650 chances over the course of a season to hit the ball for a base hit. To hit a respectable .300, a batter must record about 195 base hits in the whole season. A less respectable .250 hitter will only register around 163 base hits. This difference of 32 base hits in an entire season is spread out over 162 games (for Major League players) and is equivalent to one extra hit every four games. If you go to the ballpark

---

[98] Blake Murphy, Full Spectrum Baseball, "Sabermetric Mining: Hitter BABIP," August 2012.

every day, you may not even notice the difference between the .300 hitter and the .250 hitter (just as one might not notice the subtle effects of inflation). Like the batter, it's important for an investor to play the percentages over a long period of time. But you can't get a hit if you don't first step up to the plate.

It's time to reconsider your batting average. In this chapter, I'll delve deeper into the role of risk in the portfolio and how its mitigation is key to long-term growth.

You'll remember that one of the tenets of Nobel Prize winner Daniel Kahneman's concept of behavioral economics is the notion of prospect theory, which is an examination of how people react to different levels of risk.[99] Prospect theory is associated with the accompanying theory of loss aversion, and with good reason. Kahneman's and partner Tversky's experiments show people value gains and losses differently. The emotional impact of a loss is greater than the emotional euphoria associated with a gain.[100] This means, quite simply, people hate losing more than they love winning. As such, individuals will make decisions involving risk based on this instinctual (and often irrational) response. For example, as Richard Thaler notes in the *Journal of Behavioral Decision Making* that people may drive across town to save $5 on a $15 calculator, but won't drive across town to save $5 on a $125 coat.[101] The outcome, a savings of $5, is the same in each case. So why the perceived discrepancy and therefore the different response? Because when it comes to money, people are often irrational.

Loss Aversion: Play It Safe

Here's another example from Kahneman and Tversky. The following problem looks at two different scenarios where study participants were given a sum of money. They were then asked questions to determine

---

[99] John Sullivan, *AdvisorOne*, "Behavioral Economics: Your Own Worst Enemy," December 2011.

[100] Laura Hoffmans, *Forbes*, "January Effect...Anyone?" January 2012.

[101] Richard H. Thaler, *Journal of Behavioral Decision Making*, "Mental Accounting Matters," 1999.

how much risk they were willing to take. It's a bit complicated, so let's break it down in the chart in Figure 7.1.[102]

It Depends on How It's Phrased...

In problem **one**, subjects were given an imaginary **$1,000** and asked to choose between:

A   A 50% chance to **gain** $1,000 or a 50% chance to gain nothing

B   A sure **gain** of $500

....

In problem **two**, subjects were given an imaginary **$2,000** and asked to choose between:

A   A 50% chance to **lose** $1,000 or a 50% chance to lose nothing

B   A sure **loss** of $500

If the majority opts for the $1,500 payout of (B) in problem one, the majority therefore ought to take the same $1,500 payout of (B) in problem two. But this did not happen.

In problem one, **84% chose (B).**
In problem two, **69% chose (A).**

Figure 7.1

Why the difference? The study participants placed a higher value on a loss than on a gain. In other words, losses figured more prominently in the minds of the participants than gains.

It's only one example, but important to our larger understanding (or misunderstanding) of risk. This type of behavior has led institutions and financial services companies to understand how important it is to investors to preserve as much of their original investment as possible, in addition to any returns. Since 2008, a proliferation of hedging strategies employed by mutual fund managers proudly trumpet that shareholders

---

[102] Dirk Olin, *New York Times*, "Prospect Theory," June 2003; Daniel Kahneman and Amos Tversky, Econometrica, "Prospect Theory: An Analysis of Decision Under Risk," March 1979.

might not experience the "high-highs" in strong bull markets, but they also won't experience the "low-lows" in terms of bear market returns.

One example occurred in 2008. In that year, the S&P 500 Index was down 37%, but hedge fund indices were only down 18%, on average, even including the high at 32% and the low at negative 58%.[103] At the same time the market was falling, a few hedge fund indices managed to eke out positive returns—a merger arbitrage hedge fund index and a hedge fund macro index, for example. Correspondingly, when the market began to increase in 2009, hedge fund strategies and investment philosophies employed by certain managers had them lagging in the recovery. Judging from the share of assets these "alt-style" funds received, some investors wanted "downside risk protection and uncorrelated returns,"[104] which I think means investors didn't mind sacrificing some of the upside potential for the possibility of less volatility and hopes of, once again, a smoother ride.

Hall of Fame: Unparalleled Returns

Let's take a look at two return approaches. Relative return compares the performance of a given investment to that of similar products, as well as the overall market. Absolute return is simply what the investment return is over a certain period. It does little good for someone who is recently retired to find the market down 40 percent, but their portfolio down by only 20%. Yes, they're certainly better off than they could be, but it's only a matter of degree. They still have less than when they started.

Chances are we all know someone who was preparing to retire during, or in the immediate aftermath, of the financial crisis of 2008. Many plans were put on hold and it quickly became apparent to some that a drastic revision of their spending projections, if not a full-blown return to work, was required. In either case, retirees and pre-retirees fell victim

---

[103] Lipper, a Thomson Reuters Company, 2013.

[104] *Financial Times*, "Mutual Funds Search for Growth in New Landscape," April 29, 2011; Post Bulletin, "Stock Market on Rebound, but Mutual Fund Investors Still Wary," September 7, 2012.

to what's known as "sequence of return" risk, which involves the impact of negative investment returns early in retirement.[105] The reason it matters is that retirees must rely on their savings to generate necessary income. If they draw on those savings during down markets, meaning they remove a portion to pay for living expenses, it will be that much harder to recover those assets when markets are good.

To better illustrate sequence of returns, let's look at an example with two hypothetical accounts representing the assets of two investors. Notice in Figure 7.2 that although the accounts take different paths, they reach the end of the accumulation phase with the same average annual total rate of return of 8% and standard deviation of 14.4%. The key difference between them is that the rates of return are inverted.

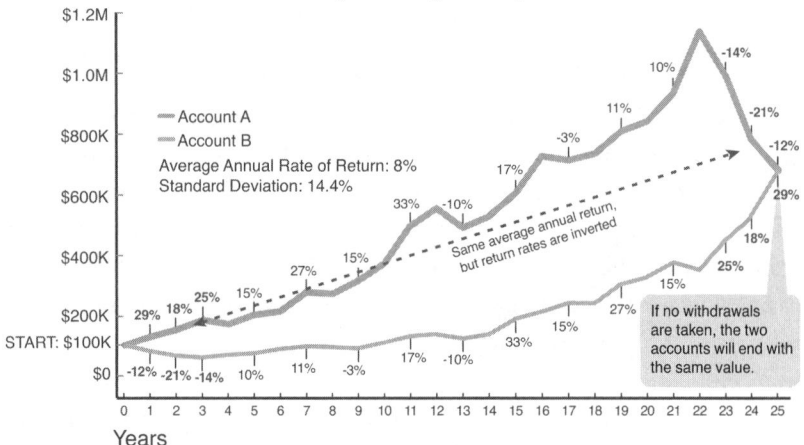

Figure 7.2

---

[105] Darla Mercado, *Investment News*, "4% Withdrawal Rule Called into Question," January 22, 2012.

Now let's look at two hypothetical accounts representing the nest eggs of two retirees. Each retiree remains invested and needs to withdraw 5% at the end of every year. As you can see in Figure 7.3, the starting point is the same for both accounts, but the end results are very different. The investor in Account A, who began the distribution phase in an up market, achieves an ending balance greater than when distributions began. But when rates of return are inverted, as in Account B, the investor taking the same 5% each year in a down market depletes the account by year 13. Now just to give you the full picture, there are discussions around what is the right amount to withdraw every year, and there is no agreement in the industry. Here I am illustrating 5%, but you need to work with your financial professional to determine what the right amount is for you.

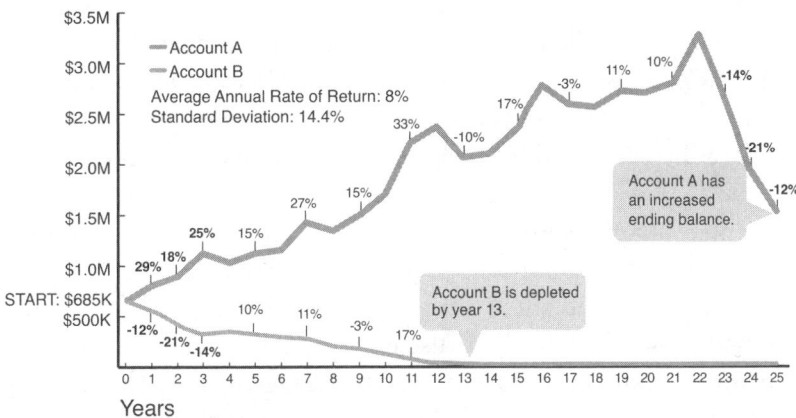

Figure 7.3

Obviously from these examples you can see how important sequence of returns are and the impact they can make in retirement. That is why in my opinion, enhancing diversification through lower correlated investments is so important.

A study in the *Journal of Indexes* further explains the benefits of lower correlation in a portfolio.

"There are several quantifiable benefits of lowering the correlation of a retirement-withdrawal-mode portfolio's component assets," notes Craig Israelsen, Ph.D., a professor of personal finance who taught at Brigham Young University and University of Missouri, and is the study's author. "First, there is a dramatic reduction in the volatility of the portfolio's performance (i.e., lower standard deviation of return). Second, there is a significant reduction in the worst-case portfolio loss, or maximum drawdown."[106] Additionally, he pointed out that performance could increase.

Invoking our sequence-of-return discussion, the study suggests that "...maximum portfolio loss, frequency of loss, and probability of recovery following a loss are quantifiable measures of the benefits of low correlation...as was shown by the mathematics of recovery for portfolios in withdrawal mode, avoiding large losses is of paramount importance."

Most interestingly, Israelsen concludes that achieving low correlation among the assets in a portfolio requires the use of assets that "may not fit the standard paradigm of a traditional retirement portfolio, namely commodities and REITs." As discussed earlier, REITs are becoming increasingly more correlated with traditional investments. This just goes to show how quickly the investing world is changing and how important it is to stay up to date.

---

[106] Craig Israelsen, *Index Universe*, "The Benefits of Low Correlation," November/December 2007.

When considering Costner's Crash Davis analogy, remember that it's about consistently getting on base, rather than always attempting to hit a home run. Alternative investments won't always knock it out of the park, but with proper guidance, they may help you advance around the bases.

From the Alt Vault: Valuable Takeaways from Chapter Seven

The emotional impact of loss for some may be greater than the euphoria associated with gain. Additionally, a misunderstanding of risk results may lead to the slow erosion of assets and purchasing power over time. Rather than big swings and more strikeouts, volatility may be managed with singles and doubles; proper use of alternative investments may help up the investor's batting average.

- Investors' perception of risk is often a one-time event of incredible gains or devastating losses.
- Risk is not always a one-time event; it could be a slow growing risk like inflation.
- Upside potential is often sacrificed for less volatility.
- Building a portfolio that seeks absolute returns may help avoid "sequence of return" risk.
- Low correlation may require the use of assets that may not fit the traditional view of a retirement portfolio, such as alternatives.

What's next: Beta blockers reduce angina and other heart rhythm disorders. In addition to its medical nomenclature, beta is a financial term related to risk and volatility, an understanding of which can help lead to better overall financial health.

Eight
Beta Blockers

Is your blood pressure rising?

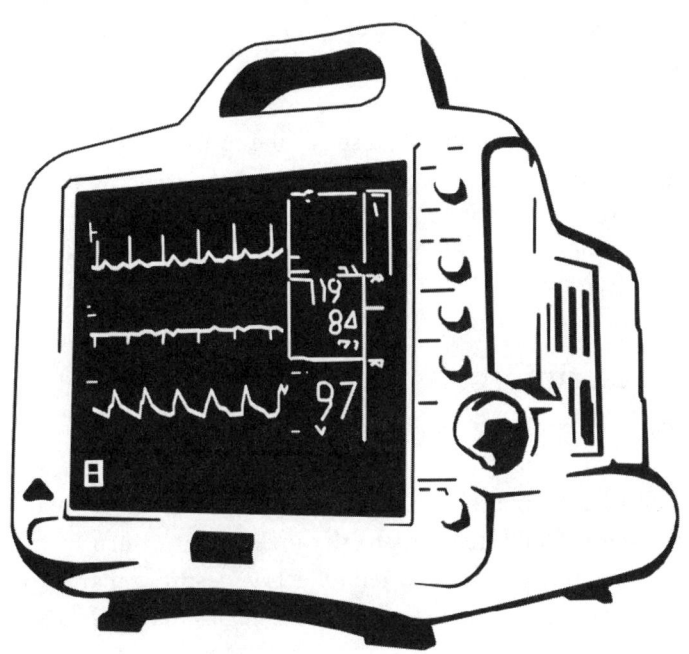

The Center for Disease Control estimates that one in three American adults suffer from the "silent killer"—high blood pressure.[107] Luckily, we have medications designed to help. Beta blockers work by reducing the effects of adrenaline, which can cause increased heart rate and higher blood pressure. Beta blockers can also help improve blood flow by opening blood vessels.[108]

In addition to its medical nomenclature, beta is also a financial term related to risk and volatility. After what could be called a global economic heart attack suffered in 2008, I feel that reducing beta serves as an appropriate metaphor for reducing the corresponding stress and angst associated with the market's peaks, valleys, and wild swings. Understanding beta and its role in the portfolio can lead to better overall financial health.

We've looked at the problems caused by living longer with fewer sources of income and increasingly correlated markets. It's now time to focus on a potential treatment by examining this important measurement of systematic risk.

The Prescription: Bringing Balance

"Past performance is no guarantee of future results."

This well-known financial industry disclaimer has taken on added significance since 2008. It refers to the investment return of individual securities and portfolios and often reflects widespread market behavior. As volatility becomes more prevalent, strategies that performed well in

---

[107] Centers for Disease Control and Prevention, "High Blood Pressure," May 2013 and Sung Sug Yoon, R.N., Ph. D.; Vicki Burt, R.N., Sc.M.; Tatiana Louis, M.S.; Margaret D. Carroll, M.S.P.H., U.S. Department of Health and Human Services, ODC, NCHS Data Brief, "Hypertension Among Adults in the United States, 2009–2010," October 2012.

[108] Mayo Clinic, "Beta Blockers," December 2010.

the past cannot be expected to deliver the same returns. Diversification, which cannot assure a gain or a loss, can help stabilize your portfolio, so that when one stock goes down, the rest don't necessarily follow.

Professor Israelsen, whom we discussed in the last chapter, has developed a multi-asset portfolio known as the *7Twelve® Portfolio*. One of his business partners, Andy Martin, explains how our understanding of diversification in a portfolio has evolved over time.

Martin points to the first balanced fund, created by CPA Walter Morgan, as an example of a key transformation in how investment managers approached diversification. The fund was eventually renamed the Wellington Fund and is still in existence today.

"There could not have been a worse time to start a stock mutual fund, or perhaps a better time to start a balanced fund," Martin writes. "The Dow Jones Industrial Average (DJIA) reaches a record peak of 381.17 on September 3, 1929, and loses 90% of its value over the next three years to a low of 41.22 on July 8, 1932. In contrast, the Wellington Fund loses 'only' 58.5%...The Wellington Fund earns a 5.9% annual return during this fateful 25 year period."[109] The fateful period that Martin is referring to is the first 25 years the Wellington Fund was in existence.

The Wellington Fund used diversification strategies to help manage the volatility of the 1930s.[110] By selecting stocks that had a low correlation to what turned out to be the Market Crash of 1929, the fund not only reduced losses but managed to achieve returns. In this case, the lower correlated stocks served as beta blockers.

In the same way the Wellington Fund used diversification to reduce beta in the 1930s, modern examples of balanced portfolios utilize multiple asset classes to enhance diversification, potentially improve

---

[109] Andy Martin, 7Twelve, "The Right Number," 2012.

[110] John C. Bogle, Bogle Financial Markets Research Center, "Reflections on Wellington Fund's 75th Birthday," 2004.

performance, and manage risk. An example is Israelsen's 7Twelve strategy (shown in Figure 8.1), which allocates money across 12 funds that fall in seven different asset categories. Strategies such as 7Twelve recognize that we live in a multi-asset world, including domestic and foreign stocks, domestic and non-U.S. bonds, real estate, commodities, and cash.[111]

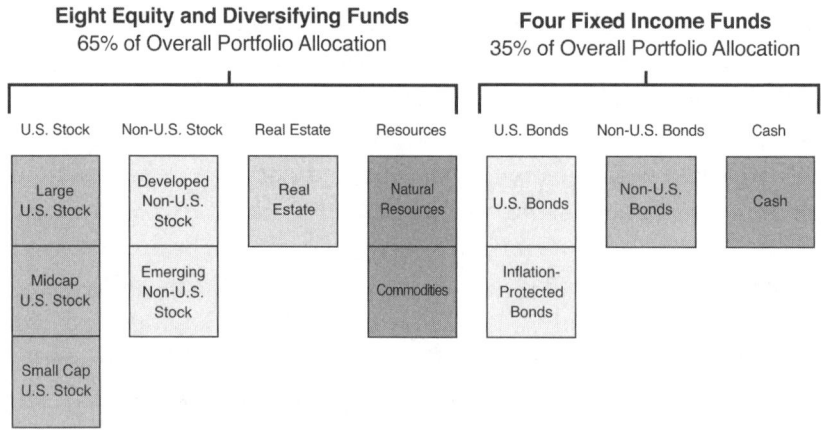

Figure 8.1

Martin says that the turbulence of 2008 taught "...us that the two-asset investment model of stocks and bonds may no longer be enough to diversify against the numerous threats to investors' security."[112] This illustrates that the right asset mix from yesterday's markets may not be the best mix for today's or tomorrow's markets, especially if one is looking to hedge against increasing correlation.

---

[111] Craig L. Israelsen, "The 7Twelve Portfolio: An Introduction," January 2013.

[112] Andy Martin, 7Twelve, "The Right Number," 2012.

Better Beta: Reduce Stress

You may wonder if there's a way to maintain your portfolio's health by attempting to maximize the performance of the individual stocks that comprise the portfolio. One option is to understand and adjust for beta, which is a statistic that compares the overall volatility of a stock to that of the market. Volatility can negatively or positively affect the performance of the stock, depending on direction. Financial professionals and money managers use beta as one of many indicators to determine investment volatility, which is a component of risk. A beta of 1.0 means that a stock's price will increase or decrease in the same direction and magnitude as the market as a whole, meaning they are closely correlated. A beta that is less than 1.0 generally means the asset has less volatility than the overall market. A beta that is greater than 1.0 means the asset has more volatility than the overall market. For example, a beta of 1.5 implies that an investor can anticipate 50% greater volatility in the movement of a stock or portfolio compared to the total market.

The chart in Figure 8.2 is a hypothetical example of how a highly correlated stock moves with the market and how volatility can have a positive or negative effect on return. When the market does well, the stock is expected to do even better. When the market does poorly, the stock is expected to do worse.

Specific to our discussion, the beta of a portfolio is a measure of market correlation and can act as a guide to better diversification. By adding together the beta of the individual securities within a given portfolio, and determining how far the portfolio is then removed from the base beta of 1.0, managers can add or remove securities to better target risk-adjusted returns.

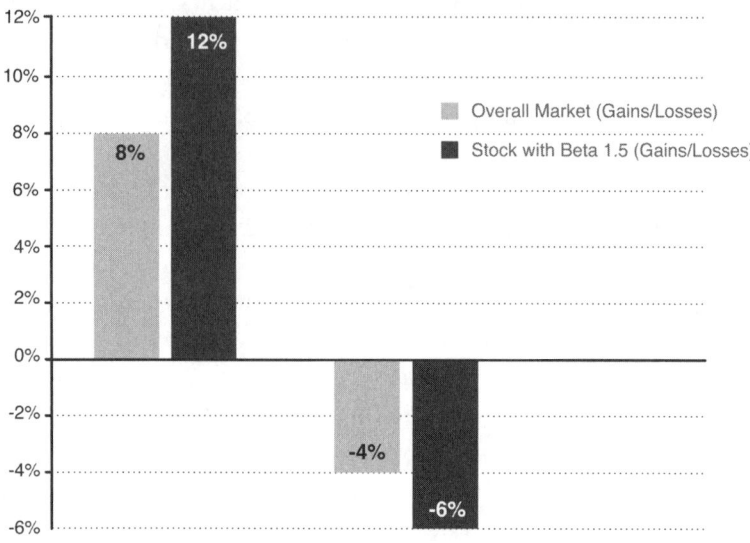

Figure 8.2

When implementing alternative strategies, beta can be reduced through greater diversification, perhaps without sacrificing long-term, risk-adjusted returns. This can enhance risk-adjusted returns and may be possible by structuring a portfolio that is focused on achieving returns that are, for the most part, uncorrelated with those of the market.

Illustrations like the beta chart point to methods to reduce risk without necessarily having a corresponding reduction in returns or, as Yale's David Swensen puts it, "by identifying high-return asset classes, not highly correlated with domestic marketable securities, investors achieve diversification without the opportunity costs of investing in fixed income. The most common high-return diversifying strategy for a U.S. investor involves adding foreign equities to the portfolio. Other possibilities for institutions include real estate, venture capital, leveraged buyouts, oil and gas participations, and absolute return strategies. If these asset classes provide high equity-like returns in a pattern that differs from the return pattern of the core asset (U.S. domestic equities), investors create portfolios that offer both high returns and diversification. Although on an asset-specific basis, higher expected returns come with the price of higher expected volatility, diversification provides investors with a mechanism to [manage] risk."[113]

Now Swenson's advice is a bit outdated as foreign equities have become increasingly correlated to domestic equities (discussed in Chapter Four). But the overall point is still valid—diversification can help manage risk. And of course, always remember that past performance is not indicative of future results.

Clinical Trial: Safe for Public Use?

Arbitrage is an alternative investment strategy that attempts to take advantage of the price discrepancy of one financial instrument available for sale or purchase in two different markets. This difference in prices means arbitrage is a "spread vehicle," since it seeks to capitalize on the difference (or spread) of the given prices.

The textbook business started by Supap Kirtsaeng is an example of arbitrage. As a student at Cornell, Kirtsaeng was shocked at how much more expensive textbooks were compared to those found in his home country of Thailand. He asked his family to send over the less expensive textbooks and sold them to U.S. students. It is estimated that he eventually netted $1.2 million, enough to catch the attention of publishers.[114] John Wiley & Sons filed a copyright infringement suit against Kirtsaeng, but ultimately lost (in March 2013 the U.S. Supreme Court overturned a

---

[113] David F. Swensen, "Pioneering Portfolio Management," 2000.

[114] Bill Hadley, UneMed, "Limitations on Copyright—The First-Sale Doctrine," 2012.

lower court's ruling that had gone in the publisher's favor). Kirtsaeng's story is an example of arbitrage, as he used the difference in pricing between two markets to his advantage.

In the investment world, arbitrage opportunities exist only momentarily, and if the strategy is incorrectly performed, can be especially devastating. Currency arbitrage trading, for instance, requires the availability of real-time price quotes and the ability to react quickly as opportunities present themselves. To determine the best arbitrage moment, some use "black boxes," which rely on proprietary algorithms for speed and efficiency to calculate opportunities in the market. [115] Of course, Wall Street doesn't rely entirely on artificial intelligence. Often a real, live human makes the final trading call.

Another example of arbitrage is a merger arbitrage. Specific to our investment topic, suppose ABC company is acquiring XYZ company. An investor who believed XYZ stock will increase in value due to the merger, and that ABC stock would drop in value, would take advantage of a merger arbitrage opportunity by buying XYZ stock and selling short ABC stock (or bonds).

> Company ABC is acquiring Company XYZ
>
> Company ABC's stock drops slightly
>
> Company XYZ's stock increases

Mergers and acquisitions occur regardless of market conditions (market neutral/low volatility/low correlation). Figure 8.3 is a graphical depiction to help you further understand the process of merger arbitrage.

---

[115] Investopedia, "Definition of Black Box Model," 2013.

Merger Arbitrage

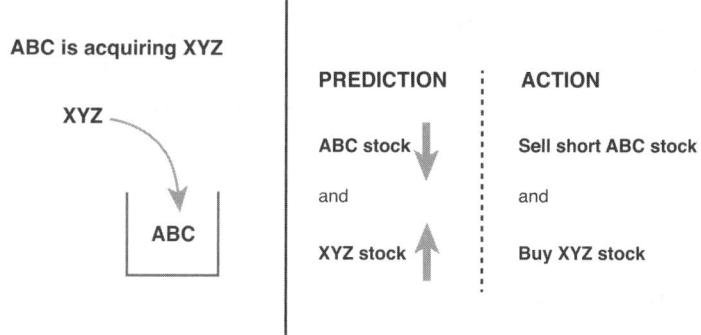

Hypothetical diagram created by Jackson National Life Insurance Company (Home office: Lansing, Michigan).

Figure 8.3

Because it involves stock markets, investors might think the arbitrage strategy is highly correlated and presents the same level of risk as stocks, but this is not the case. By being long one stock (owning the stock you expect to increase) and short another (selling the stock you expect to decrease) in equal magnitudes, market risk may be reduced. In the diagram above, the investor would buy the XYZ stock because it is expected to go up, while simultaneously selling the ABC stock because it is expected to go down. As a result, arbitrage has a low beta connection with stock markets themselves, even though they may use stock spreads (or differences) as the underlying investments. For example, the data shows that arbitrage has mid-single-digit returns and low volatility when the HFRX Merger Arbitrage Index is used as a proxy for arbitrage.[116]

---

[116] Lipper, a Thomson Reuters Company, 2013. Arbitrage returns measured by using the HFRX Merger Arbitrage Index from the index's inception of 1/30/1998 to 12/31/2013.

It is important to keep in mind that this is an investment and may lose value. In a merger arbitrage transaction, an investor could lose value from both the long and short positions held. Holding a long position, or owning a security, is a traditional investing strategy and comes with the risks typically associated with investing. A short sale may be affected by selling a security that the fund does not own. If the price of the security sold short increases, the fund would incur a loss, as the investor was expecting the price to fall; conversely, if the price declines, the fund will realize a gain.

Like all sophisticated strategies, arbitrage requires education and expertise in order to successfully execute. While in theory arbitrage is often thought of as risk-free, in practice risks abound—some are minor, such as mistiming a trade that erodes the spread (and therefore the expected return) and some can be major.

Risk Parity

Another category that potentially manages risk is a concept known as risk parity. Risk parity is all about diversification. Rather than focusing on how specific dollar amounts are spread across a portfolio, it instead involves the allocation of risk across various components in a portfolio. Risk parity means that the balance is focused on the allocation of risk, not the allocation of capital. The strategy usually involves four main drivers: equity risk, credit risk, commodity risk, and interest rate risk. Balancing the portfolio's risk across these four drivers is needed to achieve parity. Think of macro factors such as periods of rising and falling economic growth and the resulting effect on rising and falling interest rates. While it's very difficult to predict when each will occur, risk parity seeks to balance risk across each factor, thereby increasing the potential likelihood risk parity strategies perform better than capital allocated traditional investments.

More simply, by focusing on risk allocation rather than asset allocation, risk parity attempts to provide a customized risk compared to the traditional portfolio allocation of 60% stocks and 40% bonds. Because of the complexity of predicting risk, risk parity strategies are not without potential for poor returns.

So, how do strategies like risk parity and merger arbitrage transfer to other markets and other strategies in the alternative space? Let's take a look.

From the Alt Vault: Valuable Takeaways from Chapter Eight

Alternative strategies can be used as a strategy to help reduce beta. This is possible by structuring a portfolio uncorrelated to the broader market, as the premise behind this "smoother the better strategy" is that it potentially could result in less volatility.

- Beta is a risk measurement that compares the volatility of a stock or portfolio to the volatility of the market. Higher beta securities and portfolios tend to be more volatile and therefore riskier. Lower beta securities and portfolios tend to be less volatile and therefore less risky. Of course investing always involves risk.

- The 60/40 mix does not always offer the optimal mix of growth and stability due in part to higher correlation and lower diversification.

- Alternatives could be an attractive consideration thanks to a history of low correlation to traditional markets, but it is always important to keep in mind that past performance does not guarantee future results, and when considering any of these strategies, it is prudent to understand how these types of securities fit into your personal risk profile.

What's next: Alternatives are receiving attention from the general public. Adding them to your asset allocation may help to navigate different market environments.

Nine
Think Outside the Style Box™

What makes a champion tick?

I am a big basketball fan and vividly remember watching Game Five of the 1997 NBA Finals between the Chicago Bulls and the Utah Jazz. Now known as "The Flu Game," it featured a weakened and feverish Michael Jordan who was advised by doctors not to play. The news was a crippling blow to a team that had already lost its series momentum, having just ceded back-to-back games and allowing Karl Malone, John Stockton, and the rest of the Jazz to tie the series at two games apiece.

Jordan decided to ignore doctor's advice and suited up to deliver one of the best performances of his legendary career. At the end of the night, he'd racked up 38 points, seven rebounds, five assists, three steals, and one block. The iconic image of Jordan collapsing into teammate Scottie Pippen's arms as the final seconds ticked away is forever embedded in sports lore about the will to succeed. Jordan and the Bulls followed up this amazing feat with another victory, making them the NBA Champions (Jordan's fifth in his career).[117]

If only we all had the drive, strength, talent and resources of Michael Jordan, in sports and life. In the investing world, we may not have Jordan-like talents, but perhaps we can all learn to follow a disciplined approach by following a similar playbook.

Boxing Out: A Defensive Strategy

How many retail investors know of Sharpe ratios, regression analysis, alpha and beta, yield curves, and so many of the other terms that money managers regularly employ? Not many, I would guess. Because of this, many financial services firms have made attempts to educate and make the portfolio selection process easier to understand. In 1992, Chicago-based mutual fund research firm Morningstar released its now famous Morningstar Style Box strategy (see Figure 9.1) to help individual and

---

[117] Jonathan Weinberg, *Bleacher Report*, "Eight of the Most Inspirational Moments in Basketball History," February 2010.

professional investors understand the differences between mutual fund investment styles by comparing individual securities they hold. [118]

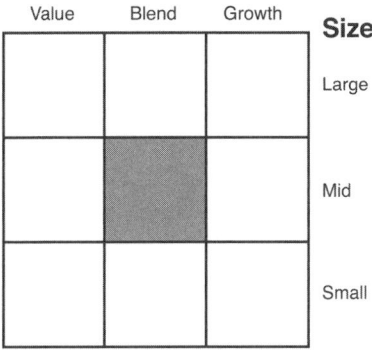

Figure 9.1

As explained by the firm, the Style Box consists of nine squares arranged on a "...grid that provides a graphical representation of the 'investment style' of stocks and mutual funds."[119] Stock funds are classified along the vertical axis according to market capitalization, while their investment style is delineated along the horizontal axis. Morningstar's definitions of market capitalization, the total equity market value of the company, split stocks into large-, mid-, and small-cap based on their relation to one another. Fixed income funds are classified along the columns according to their credit quality and classified along rows according to their sensitivity to interest rate changes. In other words, Morningstar combines credit ratings assigned (for example, by Standard and Poor's or Moody's) for each bond within the fund with the default-rate curve to display weighted-average credit quality for the fund on the vertical axis, and on the horizontal axis is how interest rate changes are expected to adversely affect the value of the fund (as shown in Figure 9.2).

---

[118] Morningstar, "Fact Sheet: The New Morningstar Style Box Methodology," 2002.

[119] Morningstar, "Morningstar Style Box," 2013.

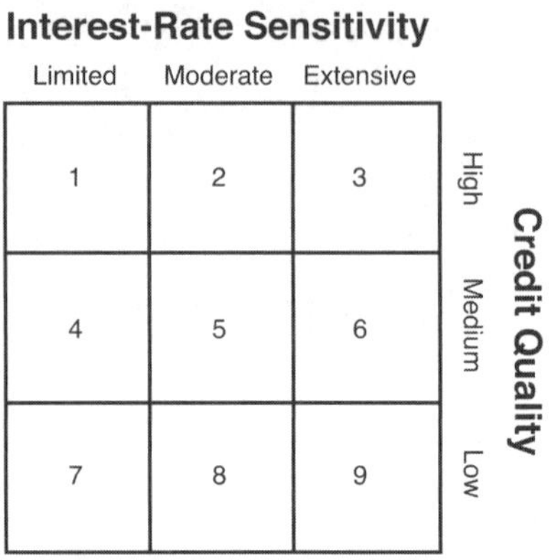

Interest-Rate Sensitivity

	Limited	Moderate	Extensive	
	1	2	3	High
	4	5	6	Medium
	7	8	9	Low

Credit Quality

Figure 9.2

With its domestic equity Style Box, for instance, a vertical and horizontal axis can be used to categorize a mutual fund into one of nine categories: large value, large blend, large growth, mid value, medium blend, medium growth, small value, small blend, and small growth. Plot it on the grid and you know into which category it falls. The idea was to help investors better understand the differences between investment styles and assist in mapping a diversification strategy.

Simply put, it's a visual aid of what can be confusing concepts that aims to help financial professionals and clients alike understand the position of a potential investment in relation to another mutual fund or security.

Xs and Os: Running a New Play

In my opinion, nine-box strategies can still work very well for traditional investment portfolios and, with a broader scope, could work for alternatives as well. I believe that adding certain alternative asset classes could help create diversification and risk-adjusted returns with lower correlation that's consistent with the investor's goals and objectives as well as risk tolerance. Examples of these possible asset classes include (across the top of the X axis, left to right):

- **Equity-based:** The majority of returns come from ownership or holding equity.

- **Inflation-based:** The majority of returns come from inflation factors or from instruments that move with inflation.

- **Absolute Return:** The majority of returns come from spreads, differences in prices, or other trends, and not on equity- or inflation-based factors.

Using data from Lipper, another mutual fund research and rating firm, I assigned various asset classes to one of the three categories of investment returns as I see them (see Figure 9.3). Then, I ordered them in order of their correlation to the general market (as measured by the S&P 500 Index). In other words, each box along the Y axis would then be less and less correlated the further one moves away from the axis intersection located in the upper left side of the grid.

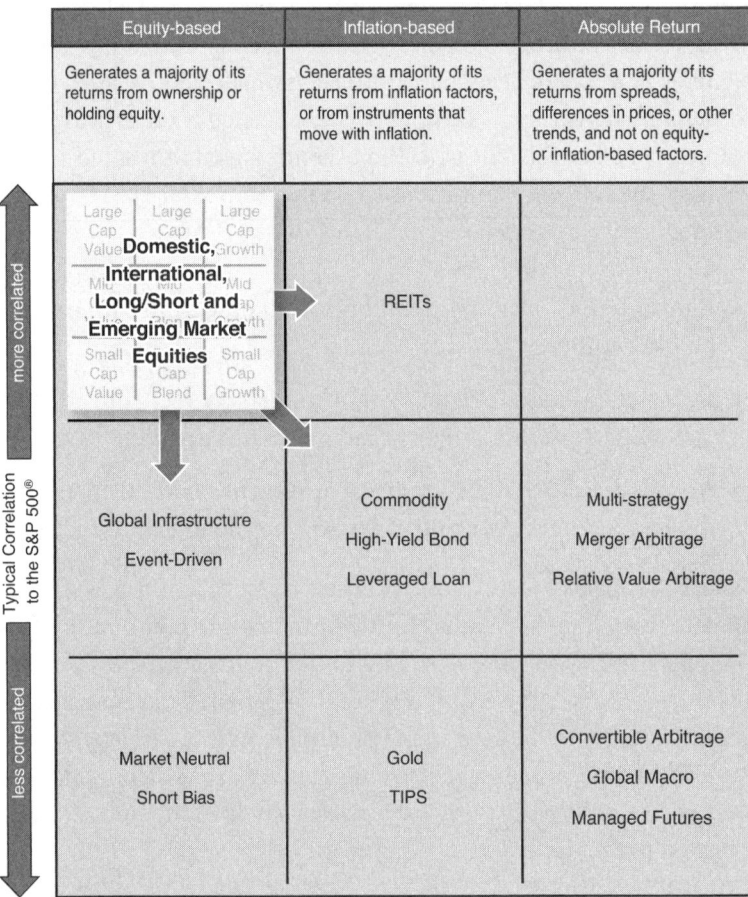

Figure 9.3

Not only does each of the examples above provide a range of lower correlations to potentially reduce overall portfolio volatility, they can also provide a variety of different sources for potential investment return.

Driving the Lane: The Importance of (Timely and Consistent) Yield

There is an aspect of investing that focuses on generating current and future sources of income, one that involves stocks and bonds. With income-generating stocks, the individual can expect a dividend, but the timing and amount of the payment is often dependent on the company's board of directors. On the other hand, certain types of bonds provide interest payments to the bondholder, which the individual expects on a quarterly, semiannual, or annual basis and, in some cases, the return of the original investment when it eventually matures.

One way to value an investment is by calculating future cash flows. For a return with relatively low risk, such as with Treasury bonds, a higher price will generally be paid by the investor, resulting in a lower yield. Conversely, higher risk is typically required in order to incur higher returns, but this also might result in higher volatility and financial stress. Additionally, yields are affected by supply and demand, as well as interest rates. As interest rates rise overall, bond prices decline, as the two are inversely related. With Treasury bonds, the Treasury Department sets a fixed face value and interest rate. If demand is strong, the Treasury bond will go to the highest bidder at a price above its face value, which means it will be sold for more than the amount on the certificate.

Stocks, on the other hand, do not carry a specified interest rate, as the potential for return comes from dividends or the stock's resale value in the market. The resale value is dependent on the supply and demand for the stock. Their dividends are not a set amount, but are declared by each company's board of directors and can differ from year to year. What happens if investors have a large concentration of assets in dividend paying stocks, or a large concentration in one dividend paying stock? The result could be devastating to the investor, and that's exactly what happened at the stock market's low in March of 2009, when a large commercial bank announced it would cut its dividend by 85%.[120] If you were a shareholder who relied on the dividend, as some shareholders did, the cut likely impacted your income. Again, we have the benefit of hindsight in evaluating their mistake; after all, it was a large and stable bank. Few saw the toll the credit crisis would exact on the American banking system. This, combined with the bank's purchase of a competitor barely two months earlier, resulted in enormous financial stress on the institution, and was the reason for the cut.

This further emphasizes the critical importance of a well-balanced and diversified portfolio. Think of investing as creating a diverse collection of cash flows that are obtained from different sources and return drivers. Recall our lemonade stand example from Chapter Five, which largely depended on the uncontrollable variables of temperature and climate in which you operate. If you only offer lemonade, business will transact mainly on sunny days. But what happens if it rains? Would offering umbrellas in addition to lemonade be a wise move? Even on sunny days, would offering sunglasses and sunscreen appeal to those who don't like lemonade?

For a real-world example, consider Google, one of the most successful companies of the Internet age with billions of dollars in market capitalization. Yet it continues to diversify its product offerings through its acquisition of the Android operating system,[121] futuristic computer glasses (marketed as Google Glass™), and even a music sharing service.[122]

---

[120] Marshall Eckblad and Mike Barris, *The Wall Street Journal*, "Wells Fargo Cuts Its Dividend 85%," March 7, 2009.

[121] Veriqual, "History of Andriod OS, from Cupcake to Jellybean," March 2013.

[122] Larry Popelka, *Bloomberg Businessweek*, "Google is Winning the Innovation War Against Apple," May 2013.

You might ask why they would diversify, as it seems unlikely the world will ever tire of search engines, or that any other website could compete. But "never say never" is a good axiom in life as well as investing. Alternative investments, therefore, are an example of tools that can help create ideas for portfolio diversification.

From the Alt Vault: Valuable Takeaways from Chapter Nine

Investors are confused about how to "get back in the game" following a period of hyper-volatility. A financial professional acts as a coach to get their clients off the sidelines. One tool at the financial professional's (and investor's) disposal over the past two decades is the Morningstar Style Box^{TM}. *I'd suggest adding alternative investments as an update for the new investing environment.*

- Good investing discipline comes from repetitive behavior. A financial professional can help.
- The Morningstar Style Box can still work well for traditional portfolios.
- A portion of your portfolio may be dependent on the impact interest rates have on financial markets.

What's next: A good portion of income is dependent on the growth of the economy and health of a company.

Ten
The Scouting Report

What's the game plan?

Finding the right players to create winning chemistry is critical to a successful season. Do you think Michael Jordan's coach, Phil Jackson, could have won 13 NBA championships and reached the levels of success he did without extensive preparation?

Jackson spent hours analyzing an opposing team's strengths and weaknesses—the areas in their playbook that represented potential problems and any weaknesses that could be exploited. Competing with and against the best players and coaches in the world meant that even the smallest detail could wind up being the difference between victory and defeat.

Since he was the ultimate "player's coach," he could relate well to the individual players as well as the overall team to get the most out of both. That meant he was often burdened with younger players without the experience and natural skill set of their large-market counterparts. Yet he was able to effectively manage the egos, immaturity, and inexperience of his players. The professional challenges Jackson faced were enormous, but he always seemed to come out on top, thanks to the mental toughness and knack for preparation he'd developed over the years.

In the financial world, investment teams at large and small firms are always looking to recruit talented individuals to strengthen their performance. Sound familiar? Each player (investment manager) is sought by these "coaches" (head of an investment team) for a specific set of skills they bring based on the needs of the team. While not all information is public, the Internet has opened up more access than ever before. Investors should try to investigate as much as possible prior to investing.

In 2010, a man named Geoffrey Lunn claimed to be Vice President of Dresdner Financial, a company that could turn an initial investment of $44,000 into $2 million in less than three weeks through its .44 Magnum Leveraged Financing Program. He was able to gain some semblance of legitimacy with his scheme by saying his company was connected to the very real Dresdner Bank in Germany. Of course, Dresdner Financial never existed and Lunn gave almost one million dollars of the money he collected to Las Vegas call girls.[123]

In late 2012, the SEC charged the purported money manager with defrauding investors in the fake company he created. "Lunn [and his partners] created an aura of credibility by inventing a fictitious firm with a name similar to a legitimate company," a statement from the SEC said. "But their 100% guaranteed investment program and the astronomical returns they promised were nothing more than an elaborate hoax."[124]

In an illustration of how even the most sophisticated investors can fall victim to the craziest of con men, Lunn told SEC investigators that he had been forced to run the scheme by a one-eyed man who threatened to kill him and his family.[125] How was Lunn able to get away with his alleged con for so long? After all, it would have required only a few phone calls to Dresdner Bank (now Commerzbank) for the fraud to be revealed.

Due Diligence: A Fundamental Layup

In the financial services industry, due diligence is a term used to describe the research and analysis an investor or financial professional will take before a financial transaction.

---

[123] *SEC News Digest*, U.S. Securities and Exchange Commission, "SEC Charges Trio in '.44 Magnum' Investment Scheme," October 19, 2012.

[124] Ibid.

[125] Ibid.

I take this to mean researching any company to the extent possible before handing over any of your money. If due diligence isn't properly performed, the investor could experience devastating consequences. Unfortunately, even if proper due diligence is performed, investors can still find themselves involved in a scam and losing money, something that was painfully apparent when the fraud perpetrated by legendary money manager Bernie Madoff was finally exposed.

The necessary level of due diligence depends on the type of investment and the person investing. Take private placements as an example. Private placement investments are often limited to certain qualified investors (meaning they must meet certain criteria, such as a minimum level of investable assets) or institutions. The due diligence for these types of investments is often conducted by specialized firms acting under specific legal guidelines. Investments seen as more widely available, such as mutual funds, have enough information in the public sphere for investors to undertake the research themselves. One consideration for an investor is to understand how the manager performed under different market conditions. One popular resource that can help with this is Morningstar's five-star system of fund evaluation. The company rates each mutual fund by assigning it a value anywhere from one to five stars. Time periods include the previous three, five, and ten years. Morningstar's system is meant to be intuitive and easy to understand.

Size and Reach: Is Bigger Better?

Due diligence is one advantage often attributed to larger money managers and their firms. It doesn't necessarily lessen the appeal of using smaller boutique firms in certain situations (those with narrow areas of expertise and experience). Yet larger firms can take advantage of their size to affect the amount of research they are able to conduct. In addition to due diligence, larger firms may offer economies of scale in other areas as well, but that is a discussion for another book.

Team Performance: Stars vs. Cellars

The stakes couldn't be higher, and money managers are often hard-pressed to repeat top performance. In fact, a study conducted by S&P Dow Jones Indices found that very few mutual funds are among the top performers year after year. Specifically, at the end of March 2013, they found that less than 5% of mutual funds were among the top performers three years in a row.[126] I think the discrepancy can be contributed to a multitude of causes, including investment objective, operations, people, and scalability.

Preparation: The REIT Way to Do It

As alternative investment strategies become more available to the average investor through retail products, how does one go about ensuring that proper due diligence is performed? While the necessary information exists, how is it accessed?

When looking at the performance history of a potential alternative manager, be prepared for a wide disparity in returns, due to the unique return structure of alternative investments. For example, a REIT (real estate investment trust) is a way for individuals to invest in income-producing real estate without having to actually buy a single, tangible piece of property. A retail investor can buy shares in a REIT that in turn invests in many different kinds of real estate. REITs could provide diversification in one's portfolio if used strategically. Yet the real estate market is not monolithic; it's regional and varies by type and investment objective. A wide swing in performance is experienced and attributed to the vagaries of the real estate market and the specific type of underlying investments contained within the REIT. Because of all this, real estate fund returns provide a historical example of return disparity. In 2011, the best REIT performers were up more than 25% and the worst REIT performers were down almost 30%.[127]

---

[126] Aye M. Soe and Frank Luo, S&P Dow Jones Indices, McGraw Hill Financial, "Does Past Performance Matter? The Persistence Scorecard," July 2013.

[127] Lipper, a Thomson Reuters Company, 2013.

Individual investors, or the financial professionals they employ to determine if a particular investment is appropriate for a given situation, may consider a host of variables, including those we have covered, such as correlation, risk, and fees. Yet other variables, often less thought about, may be considered as well, including the on-time reporting of performance and taxes. Another consideration is the alternative investment manager's performance and experience within the industry. Is the manager transparent about the process he's developed and his own history and tenure in the business? Whether or not these answers are satisfactory, and how easy they are to find, are early indications of the manager's style and philosophy.

Expensive Egos: Managing the Managers

What level of access and information are financial professionals able to receive from prospective money managers with whom they are looking to invest their client's money? A number of issues arise when attempting to gain such access, one being time constraints. There simply are not enough hours in the day for a manager to meet personally with each financial professional or large investor, so time is usually reserved for those with assets over a certain amount. So how do new financial professionals, or even the retail investors themselves, perform due diligence prior to selection?

One option for the financial professional is to hire third-party providers who specialize in performing due diligence on all sorts of companies and investment managers. For a fee, the information is collected, made available, and easy to sort and digest with the right amount of time and personnel. Large companies exist that can provide wide swaths of information, as do smaller boutique firms with a narrow, more specialized focus on just one sector or industry. It would be difficult for an average retail investor to complete this type of due diligence process without a financial professional. Consulting a financial professional is one way. Not only can a financial professional try to break you of bad investing habits while instilling good investing habits, they're familiar with the due diligence process. In fact, it is their responsibility to determine what investments are suitable for their client's specific situation.

Individual investors may want to consider the following method to evaluate an alternative investment manager (and the manager's strategy): scrutinize the manager through the lens of your goals, rather than against a standard investment benchmark performance. I always point to Warren Olsen's six "Ps" when providing examples of these criteria: product, people, philosophy, process, period, and performance.[128]

From the Alt Vault: Valuable Takeaways from Chapter Ten

Investing without the proper preparation is not usually a good choice. Due diligence is a process to research and evaluate money managers. The level of due diligence may depend on the investment type.

- A host of variables may be considered to determine the appropriateness of a particular investment.

- Transparency and a repeatable process are early indications of an investment worth considering.

- Professional help in the form of a financial advisor is strongly recommended.

What's next: Money managers who employ alternative investment strategies, similar to those that were once reserved for high-net-worth investors, are finding ways to bring them to the average investor. What's driving the change and how are these strategies accessed?

---

[128] Warren Olsen, *Business Journal*, "Wealth Management Should Start with the 6 Ps," March 27, 2005.

Eleven
Survival of the Fittest

Are you a striped beast or a flightless fowl?

Panoramic, slow motion shots of the majestic zebra charging across Africa's Serengeti, common in many nature documentaries, rarely take note of ostriches lurking just off camera, but they're often nearby. The flightless fowl has a poor sense of smell and diminished capacity for hearing, a definite liability in the environs in which it exists. It therefore relies on the zebra's movement to alert it to immediate danger. However, the ostrich's eyesight is particularly coveted by the striped beast, whose ability to see a great distance is considered poor by survival standards. For this reason, the very different, yet extremely compatible creatures move in tandem, relying on each other's strengths while accounting for each other's weaknesses. The result is a better chance for both species to survive and thrive in the harsh African wilderness.

Nature, in this case, is an apt analogy for the increasing compatibility between financial professionals who recommend alternative investments and the clients who invest with them. Metaphors that reference the animal kingdom are routinely used in investing, such as, "bull and bears," "Making a killing in the market," and "It's a jungle out there." I believe this analogy is particularly relevant in the case of financial professionals and retail clients, as each has strengths and weaknesses that complement each other and help both survive and thrive in the often harsh market environment.

Specifically, we've discussed at length how alternative investment strategies, similar to products once reserved for sophisticated, high-net-worth individuals and institutions, are now more available to retail investors in a different way, meaning through different vehicles. It's a question of how these sophisticated strategies can be repurposed in retail investment products for the use of the general investing public. Until recently, alternative investment managers had little incentive to make them widely available because the products would need to be registered and therefore subject to different and potentially greater regulation. Strategies employed by alternative investment experts such as hedge fund managers were typically subject to less regulation than their retail fund manager counterparts, even though they were still subject to regulators and audits.

This was allowed because hedge funds were subject to private placement rules under Regulation D of the Securities Act of 1933. Regulation D (commonly called Reg D) contains certain rules that provide exemptions from registration requirements, allowing companies that meet these exemptions to offer and sell their securities to accredited investors without having to register the securities with the SEC.[129]

To comply with the regulations, hedge funds generally offer their securities solely to accredited investors—those who are qualified. An investor who is defined as "accredited" is either someone with a net worth (or joint net worth with their spouse) that exceeds $1 million—a person with income exceeding $200,000 in each of the two most recent years or joint income with a spouse exceeding $300,000 for those years (and the expectation that the income will remain the same for that year). In addition, a trust with assets in excess of $5 million that was not formed with the sole intent of acquiring the securities offered is also defined as an "accredited investor."[130]

Hedge Funds: Asset Hunters and Gatherers and More

But in the wake of the economic crisis, hedge funds, like almost every other sector of the financial services industry, saw their registration and reporting requirements modified. In 2010, new laws were passed in the European Union and U.S. which (among other changes) introduced new hedge fund reporting regulations. The Dodd-Frank Wall Street Reform Act was signed into law in the U.S. in July 2010, and contains provisions which require hedge fund managers with $100 million or more in assets to register with the SEC, loosening their regulations.[131]

---

[129] Securities and Exchange Commission, "Regulation D Offerings," December 2009.

[130] Securities and Exchange Commission, "Accredited Investors," July 2012.

[131] Managed Funds Association, "Hedge Funds and Dodd-Frank Reform," 2013.

Additionally, a smaller pool of investors is available to hedge fund managers than their retail counterparts due to inability to meet accreditation requirements and the high minimums required in order to invest. Many hedge funds are known to charge a percentage fee on assets managed, as well as a share of the profits they generate, often as high as 20%. For example, say the hedge fund charges a fee of 2% on assets managed plus a 20% share on the profits generated. In industry terms, this is known as "2 and 20." Most hedge funds put limits on the advisory fee in the form of a "high-water mark." These funds charge performance incentive fees only when the investors are experiencing a new high on the original investment called a "high-water mark." I've seen instances where hedge funds are too far away from their high-water mark to make any sizable performance fees in the near future.

Why would investment managers possibly want to offer their strategies to a sector of the market—retail investors—with different regulations and lower fees? Easy—for the access to the pool of investors that the retail market offers. That access can come from a company with a large retail distribution strategy in place, one that targets retail investors. It can offer the money manager an asset gathering sales force at a lower cost structure. In return, the company gets access to sophisticated money management strategies, which it can then offer its investors. This type of symbiotic relationship may reduce fees normally charged by high-end money managers, making the type of strategies once reserved for accredited investors more accessible and cost effective for the general public. Albeit, as I have already pointed out, hedge funds do still have high fees associated with them.

To better illustrate the point, think of a timeshare ownership or rental arrangement. A timeshare is a property with a specific ownership and use structure, one based on temporary occupancy. Multiple parties purchase the right to use the property, typically a condominium, for an allotted period of time. Although the owner purchases the time at a designated destination property, they most often do not purchase the property itself.

The developer of the destination property, often in resort areas with high real estate values, would need to target individuals with a correspondingly high net worth in order to sell their inventory outright. By splitting the rights to the unit into periods of time, they are able to widen the pool of potential buyers, and often sell individual weeks for more than the sum of the property if it was instead sold to only one party.

Specifically, in the "right to use" vacation interval option, a developer owns the resort, which is made up of condominiums or units. According to the Federal Trade Commission, each condo or unit is divided into "intervals"—either by weeks or the equivalent in points.[132]

"You purchase the right to use an interval at the resort for a specific number of years—typically between 10 and 50 years. The interest you own is legally considered personal property. The specific unit you use at the resort may not be the same each year. In addition to the price for the right to use an interval, you pay an annual maintenance fee that is likely to increase each year."[133]

Just as the developer looks for many timeshare owners with a smaller amount of net worth and income rather than a few that are of a high net worth, so too does an investment manager look to many smaller retail investors through established distribution infrastructures in order to invest in his fund.

Alternative Investments: Global Migration Patterns

Beginning with the financial crisis of 2008, research and consulting firm McKinsey and Company researched and discovered that by the end of 2011, the total amount allocated to alternative assets reached $6.5 trillion. This was a growth rate more than seven times faster than

---

[132] American Resort Development Association, Federal Trade Commission Consumer Information, "Timeshares and Vacation Plans," July 2012.

[133] Ibid.

traditional asset classes.[134] And this growth was expected to continue, fueled by increasing allocations by institutional investors and the movement of alternatives into retail investments. Unfortunately, large-scale research such as the McKinsey report is not repeated every year, but there are indications from research discussed previously that the trend may be continuing.

"By 2015, retail alternatives are expected to account for one-quarter of retail revenues (even allowing for declining revenue yields) and a majority of revenue growth as retail investors, confronted with volatile financial markets and the underfunding of their own retirements, follow the path blazed by institutional investors," McKinsey reported. "Fueling this trend is a shift in investment frameworks from relative to absolute return and a convergence of traditional and alternative asset classes, investment managers, and products."

The trend is fueled by investment managers who make the products "...more accessible, packaging alternative investment strategies into regulated mutual funds and ETFs...and selling them through traditional retail distribution channels," McKinsey notes. "As a result, retail alternative assets and alternative-like strategies such as commodities, long-short products, and market-neutral strategies have grown 21 percent annually since 2005 and now stand at roughly $700 billion, or approximately 6 percent of total U.S. long-term '40 Act retail assets."[135]

In the interest of balance, I must note that endowments overall have shifted some of their assets out of alternative investments and into equities, due largely to the stock market's performance in 2013. For instance, the Yale Investments Office, which is considered a pioneer in allocating large percentages of an endowment to alternatives, reduced its private

---

[134] McKinsey.com, "The Mainstreaming of Alternative Investments Fueling the Next Wave of Growth in Asset Management," June 2012.

[135] Ibid.

equity policy benchmark from 35% to 31% for this fiscal year, the first such reduction since 2005. However, this is seen as a tactical shift due to short-term market conditions and not a signal of a larger trend.[136]

From the Alt Vault: Valuable Takeaways from Chapter Eleven

Certain animals rely on one another to compensate for areas of weakness that threaten their survival. Investment managers and product distributors rely on each other to build their businesses. This is done by providing strategies and access to a large base of smaller retail investors. An increased pool of potential assets is their payoff.

- Compatible relationships occur in nature and investing.
- As with timeshares, average investors can pool resources.

What's next: Optimizing a portfolio's performance while insulating it from a potential downturn is a delicate balance. Getting it right involves accuracy, precision—and alternative investments.

[136] Tim Sturrock, *FundFire*, "Endowment Returns Strong, Alts Allocations Drop," November 2013.

Twelve
Fast and Furious

Are you headed for the wall?

A racecar driver's success depends on the performance and safety standards of the chosen vehicle, but there's only so much a seat belt and other safety features can do. For obvious reasons, it's critical to find a balance between the thrill of a high-speed race and careful driving. David Pintaric knows this first hand.

The president of WRP Investments in Youngstown, Ohio, also happens to race high-end sports cars in his spare time, and is currently racing on the same circuit that once counted the late actor and car enthusiast Paul Newman as a driver.

On May 12, 2012, the Dodge Viper he was driving left the track, hit a cement barrier, went end over end multiple times, and skidded to a halt, only to then be struck by another car.

> "It was the scariest moment of my life," Pintaric said.[137]

Although knocked unconscious and taken to the hospital, he walked away without a scratch. It's a moment he now shares with thousands of others, as the video of the horrific crash and seemingly miraculous aftermath has gone viral on YouTube. He credits the right equipment and a top-notch crew with saving his life, and the crash is something experts now examine to improve car safety and design.

> "In retrospect, there's a lot to be said for the engineers," he says. "They saved my life. I'm sure they went through some computer modeling, and although they probably didn't want real world experience, I was able to provide it for them."

---

[137] John Sullivan's interview with David Pintaric, June 2013.

The optimization of car and engine is what kept him safe and ready to race another day, Pintaric adds. And he now has a metaphor at the ready when discussing the value of alternative investments with his clients.

> "The engine and the portfolio have to be finely tuned in order to run smoothly," he relates. "Both have to be firing on all cylinders in order to get to the desired goal. And, importantly, both should be modified to meet whatever conditions, market or weather-related, that might suddenly appear. [Caution], in both cases, is obviously paramount."

We will now turn to balancing risk and return potential within the alternative portfolio.

Post-Modern Portfolios: Revving the Engine

I've talked about how traditional tenets of investing, such as the efficient frontier and modern portfolio theory developed by Dr. Markowitz, aren't necessarily wrong, it's just that too many financial professionals and investors may fail to consider the latest variables and solutions available. In other words, your current car might drive just fine, but could a new model offer more fuel efficiency or stereo features that better fit your needs? However, at the same time, could the speeds the new car is able to reach endanger the driver and passengers?

Like a car, an optimal portfolio is created by combining assets that complement one another and help address a number of variables, including volatility. As seen in earlier chapters, adding alternative investments to the portfolio has historically been shown to improve risk-adjusted returns. While there is no guarantee they will do so in the future, depending on the combination of investments, the mix can impact risk, return, or some combination of both.

The right mix of risk and reward for a given market environment would result in optimal portfolio performance, just as the right combination of safety measures could increase Pintaric's chances for a safe and winning ride. Unfortunately, a perfectly safe car, just like the "optimal" portfolio, does not exist. Similarly, investors always face the risk of poor returns despite the precautions they take. Does this mean everyone should avoid investing entirely? Not at all. It simply means that as new developments and strategies are introduced, it's worth it to take a look.

Getting Tactical: Rotate the Tires

As I mentioned briefly in the book's introduction, the general concept of buy-and-hold, as a singular strategy, is not as effective as it once was, quite simply because of an increase in the number and volatility of the variables that potentially affect a portfolio. That doesn't mean, however, that constantly reacting to threats and opportunities in an effort to time the market is any better. A fine line exists between selling too soon and holding too long. What are some signs that an investment is underperforming? What are the metrics used to identify said underperformance, and how long is too long to stick with it?

Money managers and financial professionals spend an inordinate amount of money and resources in an effort to answer these very questions and involve what are known as tactical asset allocation strategies.

Tactical asset allocation involves the shifting of the percentages of various asset classes within a portfolio depending on the attractiveness of various markets. Alternative investment managers can be evaluated through two lenses on how well they execute a tactical rotation strategy—their investment reasoning and corporate governance.[138]

---

[138] Interview with Brian Hargreaves, Vice President of Alternative Investments, Curian Capital, 2013.

Investment reasoning involves a close examination of the manager's performance through various market cycles, whether it's volatile equity markets, a disruptive event involving the credit quality of fixed income markets, or confusion over interest rates and the direction they may take in the near future.[139] What does the manager's performance look like throughout each, and what active changes do they make to the exposure in the portfolio? Investment managers are rarely evaluated on a one-month, six-month, or even one-year basis, as time is needed for the investment reasoning to play out. For example, gold can be a volatile investment. A manager of a gold commodities fund might therefore lose 20% within a given time frame, but if that timeframe is short enough, he might still be operating within the mandate for which he was hired, and a 30% gain from the pre-drop price might be close behind.

Corporate governance involves an evaluation of items such as portfolio management turnover, operations and compliance errors, and changes to ownership structures and the management companies. Any and all could be distractions that have an impact on performance.[140]

How nimble or steadfast the manager or advisor is in replacing investments is key to a successful tactical rotation strategy. Like tires on a car during a race, replace too soon and it's wasted time and money; replace too late (or not at all) and disaster could strike.

---

[139] Interview with Brian Hargreaves, Vice President of Alternative Investments, Curian Capital, 2013.

[140] Ibid.

Alternative Investments: Riding an Annuity Chassis

I've mentioned mutual funds, managed futures, and exchange traded funds, among others, as examples of products that provide access to the alternative investment space. There's another product that isn't associated with terms like "cutting edge" and "innovative" in the public lexicon, so it doesn't immediately come to mind when thinking about alternative investments, yet it offers access nonetheless. More and more variable annuities are adding alternative investment products to their subaccount options because of the benefits of combining the two. Variable annuities are insurance contracts in which the value of the investment portion fluctuates based on underlying subaccounts. Investments made in the subaccounts accumulate tax free and can be withdrawn without penalty beginning at age 59½. Taxes are then paid on the capital gains of the investments, but not the amount of the original investment, known as the investment basis.

In recent years, variable annuities have focused on addressing the need for guaranteed sources of income in retirement through what are known as living benefit riders that are attached to the annuity contract. These guarantees are backed by the insurance company issuing the contract. Annuity owners accumulate wealth with the power of tax deferral, meaning that they do not have to pay taxes until they take the money out of the annuity. They can then partially choose how best to distribute their accumulated, tax-deferred gains, subject to their individual situation and certain provisions that can vary based on the annuity provider. These living benefit riders, combined with an increasing number of subaccount options (or the underlying investments in which the annuity assets can be invested) led to an explosion of industry growth in the 1990s and 2000s.

Before investing, investors should carefully consider the investment objectives, risks, charges, and expenses of a variable annuity and its underlying investments options. The current contract prospectus and underlying fund prospectus which are contained in the same document provide this and other important information. Please contact your representative or the company to obtain the prospectuses. Please read the prospectuses carefully before investing or sending money. Optional benefits are available for an extra charge in addition to the ongoing fees and expenses of the variable annuity. The long-term advantage of the benefit will vary with the terms of the benefit option, the investment performance of the variable investment options selected, and the length of time the annuity is owned. As a result, in some circumstances the cost of the option may exceed the actual benefit paid under the option.

Annuities focus on tax deferral and providing steady streams of income. Recently for many investors, diversification increasingly became a concern, and demand grew for products that could help address the concern.

Because alternative investment strategies can potentially generate high trading activity and in turn generate tax ramifications for investors, investing in a tax-deferred vehicle like an annuity may benefit the investor (it is important to also recognize that losses can still occur including loss of principal).

For this reason, insurance companies are partnering with asset managers and alternative investment specialists to package products that can potentially meet a variety of investor risk tolerances in a tax-deferred environment.

Portfolio Optimization: Balancing Risk and Return

Alternative investments work well as a diversifier, but I don't believe they should be used to the exclusion of other investment vehicles; they are a tool that could help reduce volatility over time. See Chapter Five for how allocations to alternative investments and strategies have historically improved returns and managed risks. Of course, past performance is no guarantee of future results.

Ultimately, the goal of an investor in constructing a portfolio is to gather assets together in a risk-appropriate combination, balancing the desire for return with their fear of loss. Each component of the portfolio plays a distinct role in that objective. At times it can be a delicate balance and, when viewed in isolation, the role of the individual asset is not always obvious. Therefore, it is best to view the contribution of any asset not in regard to its individual performance, but in terms of how it has enabled the portfolio in aggregate to accomplish a suitable risk/reward profile for the investor.

Portfolio Overlay: Understanding the Diagnostics

One critical point I emphasize about this chapter (and indeed the book) is the importance of overlay management. Just as engine components must harmonize to function efficiently, so too do the various components of a portfolio. Any adjustments to the portfolio are evaluated through the overlay system, meaning in total, and their effects on each individual position are then analyzed. In other words, balance and coordination among multiple separate account managers is the key. Disconnected pieces of a portfolio are integrated into a single account so a single investment solution is ultimately implemented. If one were to overload a number of alternative investments without some type of overlay system, it could potentially destroy value.

It is no different than with traditional investments, where investors want to ensure their mutual fund investments don't overlap with one another and/or with their individual stock and bond investments. It also involves an understanding of how the components of the portfolio are correlated, whereby it has the lowest standard deviation possible while seeking the greatest return possible on an ongoing basis with the end investor's interest in mind. I believe the importance and value of overlay management cannot be overemphasized, and as we discuss various alternative strategies and structures in the following chapters, it will become apparent why.

From the Alt Vault: Valuable Takeaways from Chapter Twelve

Designing a suitable portfolio can be challenging because of the sheer number of investment choices. On top of that, even if done correctly, inefficiencies can be introduced that drag on performance. Financial professionals can help.

- The portfolio, like a highly-tuned engine, must regularly be tuned up to ensure suitability.
- Variable annuity products may offer access to alts in a tax-deferred framework.
- Financial professionals can help achieve a suitable portfolio.

What's next: While not without risk, leverage can be added to alternative investment strategies. Once reserved only for qualified investors, financial services companies are packaging similar such investment strategies into product structures and vehicles that individual investors can use. But what are those investment strategies, how are they used, and what are the specific strategies employed?

Thirteen
How Leverage Works

How do you move a mountain?

In days of yore, prior to the industrial age, a block and tackle pulley system proved to be an effective method to lift a heavy load. Even with the advent of backhoes, bulldozers, and other modern machinery, this ingenious device can still be found combating the laws of physics today. If you've ever seen (or used) an engine lift or the rigging of a sailboat, you've witnessed a block and tackle system. A combination of strategically placed ropes and pulleys evenly distribute weight in a manner that allows an individual or group to lift a load far beyond what their strength and numbers would otherwise deem possible. Simply put, the more pulleys employed, the more evenly the weight is distributed, and consequently, the easier it is to lift a desired item. While the objective is to lift the load, the block and tackle system uses leverage to do the job. Leverage in this case is defined as moving an object from point A to point B by using force.

With investing, the term *leverage* refers to a strategy that uses borrowed money to either purchase securities, invest in businesses, or generally seek a return higher than would have been received had the money not been borrowed. As an example, a new business will borrow money from the bank to cover start-up costs. Once the business begins to turn a profit, the loan is paid back. Although the company no longer has that initial lump sum of money, the owner now has a business that hopefully will continue to produce positive returns. Like a heavy load that requires additional force through a block and tackle system, so it is with the help of a lender to increase buying power. However, a strong note of caution, just as leverage can be used to enhance return, it can—and does—magnify volatility, which in turn can magnify losses, meaning someone can lose far more than their original investment.

We've previously discussed concepts such as correlation, volatility, market exposure, and beta as influencing factors of investment risk and return. We will now take a look at another factor—leverage. Leverage is created using certain strategies that seek to amplify returns (either negatively or positively). However, as I noted above, I've seen it repeatedly misused, which can result in increased volatility and often devastating consequences.

The Mortgage Industry: Strawberry Fields Forever

The misuse of credit and leverage are central causes of recent mortgage industry woes of the late 2000s. Nowhere was this better illustrated than with the plight of two strawberry workers, a husband and wife, who attempted to achieve the American Dream in part through home ownership. In the spring of 2007 the *San Francisco Gate* reported the story of Alberto and Rosa Ramirez.[141]

The couple worked in the fields in and around Watsonville, California, and earned a combined income of $31,200 a year. In 2006, they pooled their resources with another couple (mushroom farmers who earned around $52,000 a year) to purchase a four-bedroom, two-bathroom home in nearby Hollister for $720,000 with a minimal down payment. Not only was the loan for more than eight times their combined annual income, the loan was only written in Alberto Ramirez's name, which meant in the end the burden of the debt fell solely on his shoulders. The couple and their lender would come to personify a mortgage industry "...too innovative for its own good," meaning lenders were becoming so creative with loans that loans were being given to people who could not actually afford them. I see the mortgage industry during that time as rife with market inefficiencies, irrational exuberance, ill-informed consumers, and all-out fraud. It's one of several stories that surfaced once the bubble burst—an example of just how over-leveraged homeowners became as the housing market quickly dropped into crisis mode.

While leverage comes with greater risks, especially when improperly used (as the example of the strawberry pickers shows), the concept can also be employed to potentially achieve positive results. But before we get ahead of ourselves, let me further describe what it means.

---

[141] Carol Lloyd, *San Francisco Gate*, "Minorities are the Emerging Face of the Subprime Crisis," April 2007.

130/30 Funds: Short But Growing Longer

An interesting example of leverage is its application within a 130/30 fund strategy. The objective of a 130/30 fund is to provide returns by using both a long and short security position. A long position is one in which the investor buys the security because he or she believes the expected value of the security will increase over time. A short position is one in which the investor attempts to capitalize from a decrease in a security's value and involves the selling of borrowed securities. The gain in a long and short strategy comes from the *difference* (or spread) in the price of the securities, rather than from the price of the securities themselves.

In simplified terms, rather than experiencing a stock's declining value, investors in 130/30 funds can potentially benefit from it if the strategy is executed correctly, as we shall see (that's a big "if"). Here's how they work, according to *U.S. News and World Report*:

> "A fund manager buys $100 worth of stocks he thinks will rise, then borrows and sells $30 worth of stocks he thinks will fall (a textbook example of "short-selling"). He uses the proceeds of the short sale to buy $30 more in long positions, leaving the fund with $130 in long positions and $30 in short positions. Subtract the short from the long and you end up 100 percent net long, although with $160 in total investment positions poised for gains if the manager's picks prove correct.

> "The idea behind the 130/30 fund is that it frees an astute fund manager from the so-called long-only constraint that applies to most mutual fund strategies. A long-only fund manager can't do much to exploit stocks he thinks will fall, except underweight (relative to a reference index, which most funds use) or avoid them altogether. In a 130/30 structure, though, managers can actually profit from shorting these stocks. Because the fund remains 100 percent net long, the theory goes, investors get more upside potential without a lot more risk."[142]

---

[142] Chris Gay, *U.S. News and World Report*, "Leverage, Volatility, and the Curious Case of 130/30 Funds," July 2012.

Even though they're collectively referred to as 130/30 funds, the ratio can actually range from 100/10 to 150/50. Whatever the case may be, it's important to note that as a strategy, the 130/30 model has had a "wildly checkered" track record. New 130/30 funds sprung up in 2007 and 2008, but as *U.S. News* notes, many closed soon after the market meltdown of 2008 and 2009.

"One thing to know about 130/30 funds is that they are not intended to provide downside protection, a tempting assumption given that they short stocks," the article reports. "In fact, a Morningstar report from April 2009 shows that ten 130/30 funds collectively did worse than their long-only counterparts during the severe bear market that had just bottomed out. The 130/30 funds fell 43%, compared with 41% for the long-only funds." This report is relevant because it demonstrates that during extreme market conditions, 130/30 funds can suffer. Contrary to their performance in a volatile market like 2008, in a bull market like 2013, 130/30 funds produced "stellar" returns, as a research analyst at Lipper, a Thomson Reuters Company, proclaimed.[143]

Leverage: Note the Danger and Look Down

The lesson to be learned from strategies that employ leverage, especially during 2008, is that in periods of high speculative returns, most investors tend to focus on the upside and not the downside (which caused so much trouble during the housing boom). A good example involves futures contracts, which typically require between a 5% and 10% upfront deposit. If the price of the underlying investment declines past a specified amount (known as the maintenance margin), the investor receives a request to deposit additional money to bring the balance back to the initial amount.[144]

---

[143] Jeff Tjornehoj, Lipper, a Thomson Reuters Company, "Are 'Alts' Making the Grade?" November 2013.

[144] Investopedia, "Futures Fundamentals: Characteristics," 2013.

I would make the argument that most financial crises we have experienced are the result of too much leverage. A retail investor can margin a stock account at a brokerage firm 2-to-1; however, just before the Great Crash of 1929, an investor could margin individual stocks 9-to-1.[145] During the economic meltdown of 2008, most investment banks were leveraged at 30-to-1,[146] which, since they employ the use of leverage, means they can magnify losses or gains. One large bank controlled more than $1.7 trillion in assets, but the market value of their stock only amounted to $169 billion.[147] In other words, this particular bank margined roughly $1.5 trillion, or the difference between the current market value of the collateral backing a loan and the face value (actual value). This equates to 10-to-1 leverage. The point to be made is that this bank controlled substantially more assets than their equity capital, meaning their vested interest in the outcome of their decisions was severely reduced. The bank itself only had $169 billion to lose, which may seem like a lot, but not with $1.7 trillion really at stake.

While all funds can be affected by declines in market value, leveraged funds, in particular, can be adversely affected because of the amount margined.

Another example of leveraged fund strategy involves 2x and 3x funds, known as "ultra" funds, which seek to return a multiple of its underlying index return on a daily basis.

For example, derivatives are one way to get leveraged exposure to an index. By buying an option or a future on a stock or an index basket you can gain leverage because only 10% down (or some other fraction) of the price is required.

---

[145] Jennifer Rosenberg, About.com, "The Stock Market Crash of 1929," 2013.

[146] Andy Singh, *Seeking Alpha*, "Leverage 101: The Real Cause of the Financial Crisis," September 2008.

[147] CNNMoney, *Fortune*, "Fortune 500," May 2008.

Ultra and 130/30 funds are examples of how the financial services industry uses leverage with an objective of generating returns greater than an underlying index. Because of their complex nature, the manager's knowledge and skill set can weigh heavily in the success of the fund. In the wrong hands leverage can act like gasoline on a fire. The key, however, to their responsible and potentially profitable use is to find that experienced manager. Of course, even the most seasoned manager can lose money.

From the Alt Vault: Valuable Takeaways from Chapter Thirteen

Leverage allows for potentially more gains or losses, and it is prudent to gain a proper understanding of leverage. The use of a qualified professional is strongly recommended.

- A 130/30 fund is an example of how a fund manager is able to own long and short positions in a portfolio.
- Leverage can be both a sword and a dagger. When an expert money manager is adept at picking winners and losers, a leveraged strategy could potentially mean a higher return than simply going long.
- Leverage should be left to the experts because it can magnify both the upside and downside.
- The problem with leverage is that most investors tend to look at the upside and don't take into account the possibility for a downside.

What's next: Hedge funds are a key structure of alternative investment strategies and a major reason for their increasing popularity.

Fourteen
Over the Hedge

How can Mother Nature help?

Since its first use in the 14th century, the word hedge has evolved into several different uses. Perhaps the most obvious use is in reference to a row of bushes used as a barrier in a garden, or even a physical fence meant to keep invaders out. Hedge has also become a verb, such as in the common phrases "hedging one's bets" or "hedging one's comments." In whatever way hedging is used, it commonly refers to a sense of defense. This certainly applies to the investing world as well, especially in the use of hedging strategies. Done right, hedging strategies are used to manage risk and still allow for the potential for upside gains, as the following story illustrates.

By now, John Paulson's almost unimaginable success is legendary throughout the financial world. One of the few people to anticipate the collapse of the housing and mortgage markets, the hedge fund manager's short selling of subprime mortgages in 2007 earned him the tag of having made "the greatest trade ever" from the *Wall Street Journal*'s Gregory Zuckerman. While others foresaw the coming crisis, many got in too early and unwound their bearish bets before the big payoff.[148] Paulson was able to convince his investors to stick by him, even though it meant long runs in Central Park to relieve stress as he waited for markets to turn. But turn they did, and the profits Paulson was able to reap are what Zuckerman refers to as "almost cartoonish" in size. When all was said and done, his New York-based firm made $15 billion in 2007. Paulson's personal cut amounted to almost $4 billion, or more than $10 million a day. "That was more than the 2007 earnings of J. K. Rowling, Oprah Winfrey, and Tiger Woods put together," Zuckerman wrote of Paulson's story.[149]

---

[148] Gregory Zuckerman, *The Wall Street Journal*, "Trader Made Billions on Subprime," January 15, 2009.

[149] Gregory Zuckerman, *The Wall Street Journal*, "Profiting From the Crash," October 2009.

Through the effective use of hedging strategies, he was one of the lucky few to profit from the collapse of the mortgaged backed securities market, and hedge funds are still relevant today. "What's more, the definition of a hedge-fund investor has also expanded to encompass regular folks with thousands of dollars, rather than millions, to spend. The progressive democratization of hedge funds opens ordinary investors to skilled managers."[150]

Hedge funds are an increasingly popular type of alternative investment strategy, but they are only one example. Other structures will be discussed further in this chapter and include private equity partnerships, public funds, and fund of funds.

Hedge Funds

The primary aim of most hedge funds is to attempt to seek positive returns in all markets with a lower amount of risk. In broad terms, a "hedge fund" is a private pool of assets that can be managed in a wide variety of methods.

A hedge fund invests in market opportunities where the manager foresees a good chance for positive returns.[151] More specific to just hedge funds, they are able to incorporate a number of different investment strategies depending on market conditions including, but not limited to, holding a short position, holding a long position, and arbitrage. Hedge fund vehicles are private, are for accredited investors, and often necessitate high minimum investments. In addition, these funds are not required to be transparent, liquid, or low cost.

While not always successful, many hedge fund managers attempt to employ a variety of strategies to quickly take advantage of market opportunities for the benefit of the fund and its investors.

---

[150] MarketWatch, *The Wall Street Journal*, "How to Buy...Hedge Funds," May 10, 2012.

[151] Magnum Funds, "About Hedge Funds," June 2013.

The following list is by no means exhaustive, but HedgeWorld[152] describes some of the differences between hedge funds and traditional mutual funds in the following ways:

Hedge Funds	Mutual Funds
Private investment vehicles	SEC registered investment vehicles
May use leverage extensively	Limited use of leverage
May engage in short selling	Maximum 30% of profits from short sales
May use derivatives	May not use derivatives
Large minimum investments	Small minimum investments
Offered by private placement memo	Offered by prospectus
Liquidity varies from monthly to annually	Daily liquidity and redemption
Manager compensated on performance	Manager paid a salary and bonus
Manager invests own capital	Manager typically does not invest own capital
Flexibility in investment strategies	Relatively inflexible
Usually aim for absolute return objective	Aim to outperform known market benchmark

It is generally agreed there are four broad hedge fund categories: market directional, corporate restructuring, convergence trading, and opportunistic. Each category is defined in the following list:

---

[152] Lipper, a Thomson Reuters Company, HedgeWorld's Education Center, Hedge Funds vs. Mutual Funds," 2013.

Market directional hedge fund strategies more closely resemble the original hedge fund definition, by virtue of balancing investments to mitigate risk and market uncertainty. Hedgefunddefiniton.com notes that directional strategies "focus on sustained longer-term gains rather than seeking to take advantage of events and changes in markets."

> "Funds using directional strategies may focus on certain market sectors, such as technology or health care, or may focus on emerging markets in developing areas of the world in order to invest in long-term growth areas. Directional hedge funds are likely to include long equity positions hedged with short positions, to cancel out short-term uncertainty. Sometimes these funds specialize in identifying and short-selling overvalued assets."[153]

"Funds focusing on **corporate restructuring** trade securities (mostly stocks and bonds) issued by companies in special situations like distress, bankruptcy, or merger," according to Macroption.com. The site explains that "...securities are often not publicly traded and there may be a closer relationship between the fund manager and the company. Sometimes the fund managers get even actively involved in the decision making inside the company during the restructuring. Common strategies include trading distressed securities, event-driven strategies, and merger arbitrage."[154]

Convergence trading is the process of trying to discover situations where two related securities are mispriced relative to one another. The relatively underpriced security is bought and the overpriced one is sold. When the price relationship converges back to "normal" a profit is made.[155]

---

[153] Hedge Fund Trading Strategies, "Hedge Fund Definition," 2009.
[154] Macroption, "Hedge Fund Trading Styles Overview," 2013.
[155] Macroption, "Convergence Trading Hedge Funds," 2013.

Lastly, **opportunistic** hedge funds are just as they sound—"investment theme changes from strategy to strategy as opportunities arise to profit from events such as IPOs, sudden price changes often caused by an interim earnings disappointment, hostile bids, and other event-driven opportunities," according to Magnum Funds.[156]

Over the past decade, hedge funds have experienced substantial growth. In fact, when you include funds of hedge funds and single-manager hedge funds (including the subset of commodities trading advisors—or CTAs), the total reported hedge fund industry amount climbed to $2.317 trillion in mid-2012.[157] Perhaps one reason is that hedge fund investment strategies can offer more flexibility than some mutual funds. In addition, a wide range of investments are available. Long-short, corporate governance funds, and market-neutral strategies could be a choices for those looking to invest in equities. And like mutual funds, hedge funds can also provide exposure to bonds and relative value, multi-strategy, event-driven, and global macro hedge funds.

Given the variety of hedge funds available, the decision to add this option to a portfolio has a number of important considerations, beginning with cost. Hedge funds have a fee structure that is considerably higher than other products. For example, many hedge funds have a management fee equal to 2% of assets and have an added incentive fee that can fall between 10–20% of fund profits achieved.[158]

Another concern for an investor and their financial professional should be the hedge fund manager's investment philosophy. Specifically, as with any investment, I believe the financial professional should get to know management's investment objective, current positions, benchmark measurement, investment process, and what is unique about the funds' approach or knowledge. Obviously the financial professional will

---

[156] Magnum Funds, "About Hedge Funds," 2013.

[157] PerTrac, "Hedge Funds Assets Continued to Rise in First Half of Year, According to PerTrac Study," August 2012.

[158] Dan Barufaldi, Investopedia, "Hedge Funds: Structures," 2013.

want to know as much as they can about anyone they trust to manage your money, so they will seek to understand the risks of the hedge funds and determine if they fit your risk tolerance.

Partnerships

A short film from Monty Python called *The Crimson Permanent Assurance* finds the employees of a venerable London financial firm turned—literally—into pirates in a sendup of the corporate raider theme common in the 1980s. The scaffolding of their building suddenly sprouts billowy sails and the stone skyscraper leaves its foundation to move about the city plundering rival investment and insurance firms. In this parody, the pirates, of course, represent corporate raiders taking over firms and liquidating their assets for profit and gain. It's a sharp bit of silliness centered on what today is commonly called private equity. Corporate raider, which was a popular euphemism for private equity in the 1980s, has softened as more retail investors gain access and favorable returns. In fact, *The New York Times* noted that "...the biggest private equity firms have made a gradual transformation that is now complete. Once known for their swashbuckling leveraged buyouts...these firms have changed into global, diversified investment companies with very public profiles."[159]

Private equity investments provide ownership in a privately held company, meaning that the corporation is not publicly traded. Because these investments can require large amounts of capital, private equity investors are often those who can make large investments in the vehicles, such as institutional investors (like banks or endowments) or the very affluent.[160]

---

[159] Peter Lattman, *The New York Times*, "Swashbucklers Transformed, and Now Much Tamer," December 2012.

[160] The Free Dictionary, "Private Equity," 2013.

The objective of a partnership is appreciation of investment capital over and above what's available with traditional investments available to the public. A partnership is a relationship existing between two or more people who enter into an agreement to carry on a trade or begin a business.[161] In this case, they invest in a portfolio of assets to achieve returns.

A very common business structure for private investors is called a limited partnership. A limited partnership is formed when the general partners and limited partners enter into a written agreement. All limited partners make an investment in the partnership and expect to receive a pre-stated share of the profits, which is ordinarily greater than the general partners up to a point, and thereafter, general partners receive less. Note that limited partners may not participate in the management decision of the partnership.[162] Of course, it is important to point out that partnerships and limited partnerships are not without risk. Limited partners encounter the possibility of "limited" losses in comparison to general partners. Those limited losses include complete loss of investment. General partners, on the other hand, are subject to potential losses of investment, claims, and lawsuits brought against the partnership.

On average, a limited partnership is expected to last 10 years, and many include a provision to extend the original period. The partners' liability is limited to the amount of their capital invested.

Traditionally, accreditation and high minimum investment requirements meant that the majority of retail investors were excluded from direct hedge funds and private equity investments. But the advent of something known as a fund of funds is granting opportunity to the general public. A fund of funds is an investment fund that allocates capital to other funds rather than to specific investments. You may also find it referred to as a multi-manager investment because the management of the investment can be outsourced to other asset managers. Venture

---

[161] IRS, "Partnerships," November 2013.

[162] The Free Dictionary, "Limited Partnership" 2013.

capital fund of funds, hedge fund of funds, and private equity fund of funds are just a few examples of the types of fund of funds available. Fund of funds offer an investor outsourcing of the daily management of capital and the investment due diligence. They are also used to add diversification to a portfolio in an effort to help reduce volatility. Among the disadvantages? Funds of funds are often subject to higher fees and investors have less control over how the capital is invested.[163]

Liquidity and Alternatives

Any discussion of alternative investments would be incomplete without a discussion of liquidity, or lack thereof. As I've mentioned, alternative investments have historically been sophisticated vehicles made available almost exclusively to institutions and qualified (read high-net-worth) retail investors. These investments were designed to be illiquid, meaning once the investment is made, the money in the investment is inaccessible to the investor until a defined period expires.[164] In order for many alternative strategies to work, they require large amounts of investment capital to take advantage of larger asset classes and security sets, as well as leverage and institutional quality managers. This means a commitment not only in the form of money on the part of the investor, but also time. If investors were to redeem their money earlier than planned, it could seriously affect the investment's overall performance, and penalize other investors.

However, the retail investor's increasing importance to alternative money managers meant a corresponding rise in alternative investment structures with more liquidity. Large amounts of capital that could be set aside for long periods of time were not a characteristic for the majority of retail investors. In order to target the demographic, a solution was needed to provide lower barriers (meaning lower minimum investment requirements and shorter time horizons) for clients to enter

---

[163] Private Equity, "Definition of Fund of Funds," 2013.

[164] Laurence Siegel, *Journal of Portfolio Management*, "Alternatives and Liquidity: Will Spending and Capital Calls Eat Your Modern Portfolio?," Fall 2008.

and exit. The results were alternative investment strategies in a mutual fund product, of which fund of funds (discussed previously) are just one example. Others include managed future funds, long-short equity funds and global macro funds, among others.

Alternative investors can now realize many of the advantages of mutual funds—transparency and due diligence, the ability to quickly buy and sell shares (often on a daily basis), and strict regulatory oversight. Of course, mutual funds come with some downside too. Capital gains are taxed, and there's the risk that the value of the investment can decline to zero.

Also, the performance of alternative investments that enjoy a high degree of liquidity may suffer. A recent study from investment firm Cliffwater LLC., a firm that provides alternative advisory services to institutional investors including endowments, foundations, retirement systems, and financial institutions, found just how much lower performance may be and why performance suffers. "Adaptation to the retail market has led most alternatives managers to modify their investment approach to accommodate the required liquidity demands from retail investors," the study reads.[165]

The study finds that alternative investment money managers with liquid products must eke out an additional 1% of return in order to draw even with their counterparts that are less liquid. For retail investors who realize the value of including non-correlated asset classes within the portfolio, but must still have the ability to access their investments (even if they never end up doing so), it might be well worth the price. However, keep in mind the prior discussion about accredited investors—not everyone can invest in all types of investments.

---

[165] Cliffwater, "Performance of Private Versus Liquid Alternatives: How Big a Difference?" June 2013.

From the Alt Vault: Valuable Takeaways from Chapter Fourteen

Hedge funds, partnerships, and private equity are examples of types of alternative investment strategies. Picking a suitable structure and product depends on your objectives, level of sophistication, and risk tolerance, among other factors.

- Hedge funds, private equity partnerships, and fund of funds are all structures that allow access to alternative investments.
- Certain types of hedge funds attempt to take advantage of market inefficiencies to deliver positive returns.
- Private equity partnerships often seek long-term appreciation in excess of publicly available investments.
- A fund of funds can pool investors' money to then invest in hedge funds or private equity.

What's Next: Regardless of the product structures, due diligence and understanding of the strategy is important. Now we will discuss some of the different alternative investment strategies that exist.

Fifteen
Strategy and Execution

What about the battle for returns?

"Audacious and profane, General George S. Patton Jr. was one of the ablest and most controversial U.S. commanders in World War II," according to PBS's *American Experience* in its description of the legendary general.[166]

As a movie buff, whenever I think of Patton I think of actor George C. Scott's Oscar-winning portrayal of the general in the movie of the same name. The real Patton, while no less colorful and aggressive, was also a master strategist.[167] I can only imagine what a great alternative investment manager Patton might have made had he chosen a different career—one in financial services. Consider the following quote attributed to the general, and how it applies to our discussion so far:

> "If everybody is thinking alike, then somebody isn't thinking."[168]

Although this quote refers to military strategy, it nonetheless applies here. The steep rise in correlation has investors all knowingly or unknowingly chasing the same opportunities, sectors and—consequently—returns. I think the herd mentality, driven by advances in communication and technology, as well as the more innate "fear of losing out," which is the emotional fuel of the stock market, has resulted in higher risk for a lower corresponding rate of return.

The importance of picking a sound investment strategy, along with an experienced alternative manager, cannot be overstated. There are managers who specialize in specific strategies. Yet it's not only the strategies (or the market) that will positively or negatively affect performance, but also the tactics the managers employ.

---

[166] American Experience, PBS, "Biography: George S. Patton Jr.," 2013.

[167] The Official Website of General George Patton, "Biography," 2013.

[168] The Official Website of General George Patton, "General George S. Patton, Jr. Quotations," 2013.

Sticking to our analogy, the U.S. Military consists of three departments: the Army, Air Force, and Navy. These are three different military structures with a common objective to defend and protect the people of the United States. During a time of war, although their strategies, tactics, and tools may vary, their end objective is to win. The success of their accomplishment will depend upon the leaders, opponents, tools and weapons at their disposal, their strategy, and probably most important, their execution. As Patton put it, "Good tactics can save even the worst strategy. Bad tactics will destroy even the best strategy."[169]

In the previous chapter, we discussed three different investment structures that utilize alternative strategies. We'll now take a deeper look at alternative strategies and attempt to bring all we've talked about together. This will entail a more academic discussion than I've previously included, but it is critically important to understand the following definitions. As such, I have included the stacked bucket art element in Figure 15.1 to make it easier to follow along. I will start with the bottom bucket and work my way up.

I like to think of alternative investments being distinguished by trading strategies (long, short, arbitrage, event based, market driven, etc). Each strategy demonstrates a risk/return characteristic influenced by the five factors (correlation, market value exposure, volatility, beta, and leverage). As an overlay to the different structures and strategies already discussed, the following classification groups have been developed. The stacked chart provides a visual representation of these classifications, which may provide a better understanding of how the various strategies relate to each other. When discussing these strategies it is important to remember that alternatives, like all investment strategies, are subject to the risk factors of their asset class, which can include general economic risk, geopolitical risk, commodity-price volatility, counterparty

---

[169] The Official Website of General George Patton, "General George S. Patton, Jr. Quotations," 2013.

and settlement risk, currency risk, derivative risk, emerging markets risk, foreign securities risk, high-yield bond exposure (aka junk bond), noninvestment-grade bond exposure, index investing risk, industry concentration risk leveraging risk, market risk, prepayment risk, liquidity risk, real estate investment risk, sector risk, short sale risk, temporary defensive positions, and large cash positions.

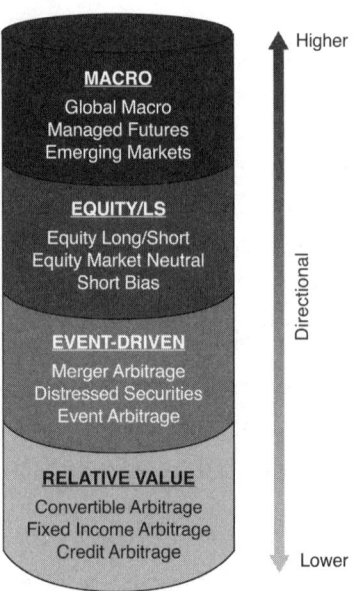

Chart created by Jackson National Life Insurance Company (Home office: Lansing, Michigan) utilizing ideas from Curian Capital®. Curian Capital is a registered investment advisor and affiliate of Jackson National Life Distributors LLC.

Figure 15.1

Now, let's list and define a number of important sub-categories, the theory being that something exists for every risk tolerance and investment objective an investor might have. However, a word of caution before we do: In the interest of balance and recognizing that each potential upside has a corresponding downside, it is critically important to understand the risks involved of a mistimed trade, the misuse of leverage, or any number of mistakes and miscues that could have a devastating effect on the investor's portfolio.

Relative Value

Relative value is the classification group found in the bottom bucket in the graphic and is a method of determining an asset's value by comparing it to the value of similar assets. It is the "... attractiveness measured in terms of risk, liquidity, and return of one instrument relative to another, or for a given instrument, of one maturity relative to another," according to Hedge Funds Consistency Index, a scholarly website dedicated to examining and educating the public about hedge funds. "The term is used in economics, business, or investment."[170]

For our discussion, relative value is an arbitrage investment strategy that buys and sells two related financial instruments, like stocks and bonds, at the same time. This allows investors to potentially take advantage of the spread (the difference in the two prices), potentially profiting from the relative value of the securities.[171] Relative value, like many of the strategies discussed in this book, is a sophisticated strategy and is inherently risky. It is important to keep in mind that this is an investment and may lose value from both the long and short positions held. Holding a long position, or owning a security, is a traditional investing strategy

---

[170] Hedge Funds Consistency Index, "Relative Value," 2013.
[171] Barclay Hedge, "Understanding Relative-Value Arbitrage," 2013.

and comes with the risks typically associated with investing. A short sale may be affected by selling a security that the fund does not own. If the price of the security sold short increases, the fund would incur a loss, as the investor was expecting the price to fall. Conversely, if the price declines, the fund will realize a gain.

Convertible bond arbitrage—Convertible bond arbitrage is a study of the relationship between a company's stock and its convertible bonds. It falls into the relative value classification group.

As our friends at Morningstar note, convertible bonds contain an option that allows the bondholder to trade in the bond for common stock at a certain price and under certain conditions.

"Usually, the bond trades for less than the stock so managers buy the bond and short the stock," the research firm notes. These strategies help manage exposure to "…interest rate risk, default risk, illiquidity in the convertible bond market, and pricing volatility in both the stock and bond markets. Because the pricing discrepancies are usually very small, many of these funds employ leverage to maximize return."[172]

However, as I previously noted in our discussion of leverage, its misuse can also lead to potentially catastrophic loss, and I'll reiterate my caution in employing these strategies.

Fixed-income arbitrage—Once again, an arbitrage strategy is simply an attempt to take advantage of any pricing discrepancy in any two markets for the same, or nearly the same, investment. This also falls into the relative value classification group. According to The Motley Fool, "…in the case of a 'fixed income' discrepancy, this refers only to bonds and related devices, since the 'fixed income' refers to the cash flow provided by an interest rate."[173] The Fool goes on to explain that for a fixed income arbitrage strategy, several things have to occur.

---

[172] Morningstar, Morningstar Investing Glossary, "Convertible Arbitrage," 2013.

[173] Walter Johnson, The Motley Fool, "Fixed Income Arbitrage Strategy," 2013.

"First, the asset involved needs to be based on interest, such as bonds. Second, the assets need to be closely related, such as two bond types that float together. Third, the sale of the asset must be simultaneous, to allow profiting from the discrepancy with little risk in most circumstances. However, high risk in rare circumstances is possible, (sic). In general, disaster can strike when the prediction of price movement proves to be false. Since most fixed-income arbitrage strategies include borrowed funds, large amounts of money can be lost rapidly."[174]

Event-Driven

Event-driven strategies are in the second bucket from the bottom in the classification group diagram. These strategies involve both long and/or short investments in the securities of corporations undergoing significant change (for example spin-offs, mergers, liquidations, bankruptcies). Hedge Fund Consistency Index notes that "such change often provides managers with a tangible catalyst by which the manager may be able to realize the expected change in value in the underlying security ...profits may [potentially] be generated by managers who correctly analyze the impact of the anticipated corporate event, predict the course of restructuring, and take positions accordingly."[175] Event-driven investments are still investments, and they may lose value. Because event-driven strategies seek to capitalize on short-term spreads, they are especially risky due to the short-term nature of the opportunity.

Merger arbitrage—In the context of hedge funds, merger arbitrage (or merger arb) involves the buying of stock in a company being acquired and the sale of stock in its acquirer.[176] Both transactions happen simultaneously. It is part of the event-driven classification group because it involves corporations going through significant change. For more on merger arb, reference the previously discussed section (and chart) in Chapter Eight.

---

[174] Walter Johnson, The Motley Fool, "Fixed Income Arbitrage Strategy," 2013.

[175] Hedge Funds Consistency Index, "Event Driven," 2013.

[176] NASDAQ, "Merger Arbitrage," 2013.

Distressed securities—Distressed securities, also part of the event-driven classification group, are primarily debt securities which originate from companies that are in the process of reorganization or liquidation under local bankruptcy law, or companies engaged in other extraordinary transactions, such as balance sheet restructurings, according to the *Hedge Fund Journal*. "A hedge fund specializing in credit is often able to purchase securities at a substantial discount to its intrinsic value."[177] Intrinsic value is the theoretical true value of a stock, which may or may not be the same as the prevailing market price. The investment is negatively impacted if the company's intrinsic value is miscalculated or the prevailing market price is never realized by the manager.

Equity L/S

An equity long-short strategy is an investing strategy that involves taking long positions in stocks that are expected to increase in value and short positions in stocks that are expected to decrease in value. As the Barclay Hedge Alternative Investment Database notes, at its most basic level, "...an equity long-short strategy consists of buying an undervalued stock and shorting an overvalued stock. Ideally, the long position will increase in value, and the short position will decline in value. If this happens, and the positions are of equal size, the hedge fund will benefit."[178] The investment is negatively impacted if either the overvalued or undervalued stock move in the wrong direction, or if the positions are of unequal size. Equity long/short is the classification group in the third bucket from the bottom.

---

[177] Thomas Della Casa and Mark Rechsteiner, *The Hedge Fund Journal*, "Hedge Fund Investing in Distressed Securities," October 2006.

[178] Barclay Hedge, "Hedge Fund Strategy—Equity Long-Short," 2013.

Short selling—One strategy that falls under equity long/short is short selling. In anticipation the market will decline, the manager sells shares that were borrowed through a brokerage firm without ever owning them outright, hoping to buy them back at a future date in the expectation that their price will drop.[179] As we discussed in Chapter Eight, short selling (in anticipation of a market decline) is traditionally very difficult for the average retail investor to execute, and usually requires a good deal of expertise.

Market neutral—Again according to Morningstar, the market neutral strategies attempt to "...[manage] the risks of the market by holding 50% of assets in long positions in stocks and 50% of assets in short positions. Funds in this group match the characteristics of their long and short portfolios, keeping factors such as P/E [price/earnings] ratios and industry exposure similar. [Individual] stock picking, rather than broad market moves, should drive a market-neutral fund's performance."[180] Yet as with other equity long/short funds in this classification group, a mistimed or unexpected move in the opposite direction of the position will adversely affect performance.

Global Macro

Returning to the Hedge Funds Consistency Index, it defines global macro funds as those that invest in markets and instruments which they believe provide the best performance opportunity worldwide.[181] I have placed this super-strategy in the top bucket in the stacked chart at the beginning of the chapter.

---

[179] Magnum Funds, "What Is a Hedge Fund?" November 2013.

[180] Morningstar, Morningstar Investing Glossary, "Market Neutral Funds," 2013.

[181] Hedge Funds Consistency Index, "Global Macro," 2013.

"At any given time, global macro managers may take positions in currencies, debt, equities, or commodities. Global macro managers may elect to take outright directional positions and, depending on their own expertise and the risk-return profile of the markets in which they are trading, they may also elect to take relative value positions—where a long position or set of positions is dynamically paired off against a short position or set of positions."[182]

Perhaps the most famous example of a global macro trade occurred in 1992. Hedge fund manager George Soros, now perhaps known more for his political activism than investing prowess, executed one of the most awe-inspiring trades in market history when he sold short more than $10 billion of British pounds. Yet it perfectly illustrates the risk and potentially negative impact inherent in this type of trade, as the entire British government was on the losing end.

Emerging markets—"An emerging market hedge fund is a hedge fund that specializes its investments in the securities of emerging market countries. Although there is no exact definition of 'emerging market countries,' these countries are in the process of developing," Barclay Hedge explains.[183] "They typically have per-capita incomes on the lower to middle end of the world range, and are in the process of moving from a closed market to an open market." Many emerging markets bring inherent political and economic instability with them, especially when compared to their developed market counterparts, which potentially could increase risk. Emerging markets funds belong to the global macro classification group.

---

[182] Hedge Funds Consistency Index, "Global Macro," 2013.

[183] Barclay Hedge, "Hedge Fund Strategy—Emerging Markets Fund," 2013.

Multi-Strategy

Multi-strategy hedge funds typically focus on between two and four of the strategies mentioned above, and generally stay with an investment theme or position longer than global macro funds. Because this strategy can combine classifications and classification groups, it is not included in the earlier stacked chart.

From the Alt Vault: Valuable Takeaways from Chapter Fifteen

Alternative investments are not as easily understood in the context of specific asset classes or instruments or structures—rather they are more easily distinguished by trading strategies. Each strategy demonstrates a risk/return characteristic influenced by the five factors (leverage, beta, correlation, market value exposure, and volatility). Ultimately each strategy is used as a component to the overall portfolio allocation, driven by its risk contribution and unique return drivers.

- The rise in correlation has investors chasing many of the same types of investment opportunities and returns because the many types of investments now move together. The psychology is likely driven by T.V. news, technology, and innate "fear of losing out."

- "Classification groups" include relative value, event-driven, equity L/S, and macro.

- Strategies generally exist for every risk tolerance and objective a client might have.

What's next: Let's put it all together.

Sixteen
Completing the Picture

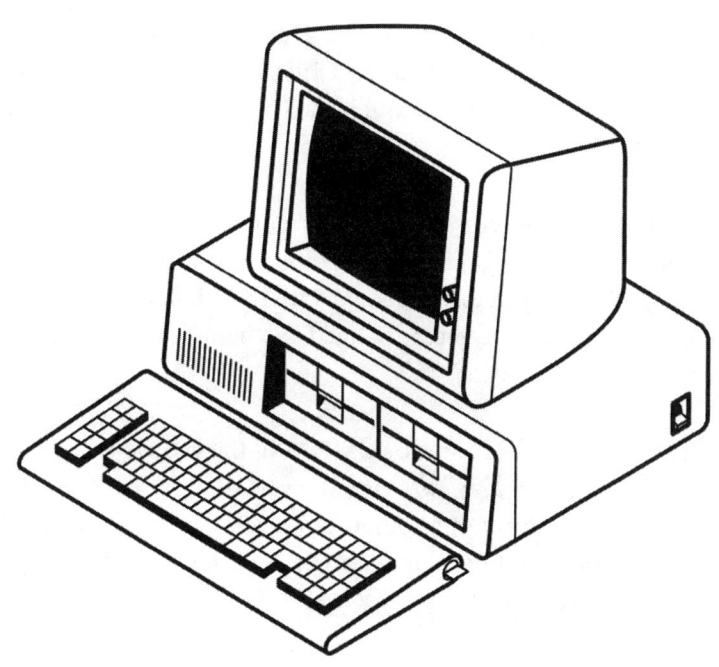

For the general population, the Internet seemed to explode from nowhere. The first time many heard of it was during a speech by then Vice President Al Gore at UCLA in 1994, which referred to a new "information superhighway."[184] Although in wide use just a few years later, the roots of the Internet can actually be traced as far back as 1962, when J.C.R. Licklider, an American computer scientist, first introduced the concept of a global network, "...where everyone on the globe is interconnected and can access programs and data at any site from anywhere."[185]

Licklider then took the lead for the Advanced Research Projects Agency Network (ARPANET), run by the U.S. Department of Defense, in the late 1960s. Throughout the 1970s and 1980s, ARPANET continued to advance, but the general public still lacked access to all the possibilities the Internet could provide.

That is until Marc Andreessen, an undergraduate student at the University of Illinois-Champaign, created a graphic browser, dubbed Mosaic, in the early 1990s. Andreessen teamed with famed Silicon Valley entrepreneur James Clark and later changed the name to Netscape.[186] The modern Internet was born.

More than 245 million U.S. residents (78% of the U.S. population) used the Internet, as of 2012.[187] As I noted, even though the Internet had been around in one form or another for decades, it wasn't accessible to the general public until developers saw a need for the technology and developed new ways for it to be accessed.

---

[184] Vice President Al Gore, "Remarks Prepared for Delivery by Vice President Al Gore," Ibiblio, 1994.

[185] Computer History Museum, "Internet History," 2004.

[186] Bio: True Story, "Marc Andreessen Biography," 2013.

[187] Internet World Stats, "Internet Usage and Population Statistics for North America," June 30, 2012.

The same can be said of alternative investments. Sophisticated strategies that make up alternative investments have been employed by a select few since the 1950s—including high-net-worth clients, institutional investors, and endowments.

Yet today, due to increases in technology and correlation and a number of other reasons previously discussed, they appeal more to the retail investor. Mutual funds, ETFs, fund of funds, and other products and strategies are vehicles retail investors can use to gain access to alternatives.

So What Now?

It isn't that alternative strategies are new. It's that new access vehicles are available to the everyday investor. As with traditional investments, some products and strategies will appeal to those with higher risk tolerances and some will appeal to those with lower risk tolerances. It all depends on the individual situation and investment objectives and how they may or may not have a place in the portfolio.

So if there is one thing to take from this book, a case has been made for considering alternative investments as a portion of the portfolio.

10 Important Points to Remember

1. Longer life spans mean a corresponding need for additional accumulation and a variety of sources of income to accommodate a longer retirement. Whereas it was once satisfied and managed by defined benefit pension plans, the advent of 401(k)s placed more of this responsibility on individual investors and their financial professionals and less on the employers. This increase in demand challenged retirement plan providers, money managers, product providers, and pretty much the entire industry to look for methods to allow investors to seek an appropriate portfolio allocation.

2. Prudent planning is no longer a luxury, but a necessity, and the process is far from easy. High correlation among asset classes in recent years means you may not be as diversified as you think. Investments that are untethered from stock and bond markets are increasingly important for two reasons: risk and return.

3. Ultimately it's about the latter. It's no longer equity versus fixed income or large-cap versus small-cap; if all asset classes become highly correlated, none of it matters. To be diversified one might consider the concepts discussed in this book—concepts such as correlation, volatility, market exposure, beta, and leverage. These are the influencing factors of investment risk and return and therefore influencing factors of diversification. When implemented, alternative strategies can help improve diversification with the potential to improve long-term returns. Remember, a proper investment strategy is not just about chasing returns (performance), it's also about managing risk. There is no guarantee that an investment strategy will be successful. Investing involves risk, including loss of principal.

4. Less volatility might be a welcome relief for investors; absent that, strategies that capitalize on volatility can be used to the investor's advantage. Globalization, growth in developing markets, and advances in communication technology masquerading as the hot, new thing have all contributed to a significant increase in volatility in recent years. So called flash crashes are an increasing and legitimate concern, and something as trivial as a false story in a hacked Twitter account can send markets reeling.[188]

5. The economic crisis of 2008 saw an $11 trillion drop in household wealth,[189] loss of savings, and an increase in sequence-of-return risk. Yet certain, non-correlated asset classes performed better than the overall market during the same period, with some performing less negatively, while others were able to eke out positive returns.

---

[188] Maureen Farrell, "High-Speed Trading Fueled Twitter Flash Crash," *CNN Money*, April 24, 2013.

[189] Emily Kaiser, "U.S. Household Wealth Falls $11.2 Trillion in 2008," *Reuters*, March 12, 2009.

6. Use of alternative strategies in a portfolio is not for everyone. Educated investors can evaluate an alternative investment manager or strategy based on their own financial goals. By constantly scrutinizing the manager or strategy through the lens of your goals, rather than against a standard investment benchmark, performance can be measured over time. If you prefer, you can always seek the guidance of a financial professional to help guide you with these important investment decisions.

7. Alternative strategies are technical, and a certain level of due diligence may be warranted. Arbitrage, or capitalizing on differences in the pricing of the same security in different markets, seems obviously technical. While commodities may seem less technical because they are goods we all easily recognize like timber, coffee beans, precious metals, and wheat, they are perhaps more complicated and may require more intensive research.

8. In the investment world, the term leverage is defined as using borrowed capital, which could also lead to the risk of loss. Like a heavy load that requires additional force (remember margin), one's financial position and return potential on investment can be similarly enhanced with the help of a lender to provide capital and therefore increase buying power.

9. But caution is strongly advised. Leverage is a strategy that can amplify returns, losses, and volatility, but often only results in the latter two. It requires a significant amount of expertise.

10. There are many types of hedging strategies: market directional, corporate restructuring, convergence trading, and opportunistic. All must be considered to ensure suitability for yourself. Again, a financial professional can help.

We could go on, but my point is not to recount the entire book; rather, it's to illustrate the importance of looking to include alternative assets in an investment portfolio. What are the goals for your investment portfolio? Is it a certain percentage return that's compounded annually, or funding a grandchild's education? Is it finding the latest investment opportunity or is it a dream vacation with a spouse? Alternative investments may help with these goals. Financial professionals stand ready and willing to help, offering expertise in a seemingly infinite number of specialty areas.

Glossary

Barclays Aggregate Bond Treasury—Broad-based measure of the investment grade, U.S. dollar-denominated fixed-rate taxable bond market, including Treasuries, government-related and corporate securities, MBS, ABS, and CMBS.

Barclays Global Aggregate—Broad-based measure of the global investment grade fixed-rate debt markets, containing the U.S. Aggregate, the Pan-European Aggregate, and the Asian-Pacific Aggregate indices, as well as other securities not contained in these indices.

Barclays Global Aggregate Hedge—Broad-based measure of the global investment grade fixed-rate debt markets, containing the U.S. Aggregate, the Pan-European Aggregate, and the Asian-Pacific Aggregate indices, as well as other securities not contained in these indices. This index is hedged to U.S. dollars.

Barclays Multiverse—Measures the performance of the global bond market.

Barclays US Aggregate Bond—Broad-based measure of the investment grade U.S. dollar-denominated, fixed-rate taxable bond market including Treasuries, government-related and corporate securities, MBS, ABS, and CMBS.

Barclays US Corp HY—Measures the market of U.S. dollar-denominated, non-investment grade, fixed-rate, taxable corporate bonds.

Barclays US Credit—U.S. corporate index and a noncorporate component that includes foreign agencies, sovereigns, supranationals, and local authorities. It is a subset of the U.S. Government/Credit Index and the U.S. Aggregate Index.

Barclays US Government—Comprises the U.S Treasury and U.S. Agency indices and also includes Treasuries and U.S. Agency debentures (publicly issued debt of U.S. Government agencies, quasi-federal corporations, and corporate or foreign debt guaranteed by the U.S. Government).

Barclays US Gov't/Credit 1–3 Year—Unmanaged index considered representative of the performance of short-term U.S. corporate bonds and U.S. government bonds with maturities from 1 to 3 years.

Barclays US Gov't/Credit 1–3 Year Yield—Nonsecuritized component of the U.S. Aggregate index and the first macro index launched by Barclays Capital. The U.S. Government/Credit index includes Treasuries (such as public obligations of the U.S. Treasury that have remaining maturities of more than one year), government-related issues (such as agency, sovereign, supranational, and local authority debt), and corporates.

Barclays US Treasury US TIPS—Rules-based, market value-weighted index that tracks inflation-protected securities issued by the U.S. Treasury.

BBA LIBOR 3 Month—Tracks interest rate at which banks can borrow funds, in marketable size, from other banks in the London interbank market. Fixed on a daily basis by the British Bankers' Association, it derives from a filtered average of the world's most creditworthy banks' interbank deposit rates for larger loans with maturities between overnight and one full year.

BofAML US Corporates 1–3 Years—A subset of the BofA Merrill Lynch US Corporate Index including all securities with a remaining term to final maturity less than three years.

BofAML US HY Master II Constrained—Contains all the securities in the BofA Merrill Lynch US High Yield Index but caps issuer exposure at 2%. Index constituents are capitalization-weighted, based on their current amount outstanding, provided the total allocation to an individual issuer does not exceed 2%.

BofAML US Treasuries 1–3 Year—Tracks the performance of the direct sovereign debt of the U.S. Government and includes all U.S. dollar-denominated U.S. Treasury notes and bonds having at least one year remaining term to maturity and a minimum amount outstanding of $1 billion.

BofAML US Treasury Bill 3 Month—Comprises a single issue purchased at the beginning of the month and held for a full month. At the end of the month that issue is sold and rolled into a newly selected issue. The issue selected at each month-end rebalancing is the outstanding Treasury Bill that matures closest to, but not beyond, three months from the rebalancing date.

BofAML US Treasury Bill 3 Month—Comprises a single issue purchased at the beginning of the month and held for a full month. At the end of the month that issue is sold and rolled into a newly selected issue. The issue selected at each month-end rebalancing is the outstanding Treasury Bill that matures closest to, but not beyond, three months from the rebalancing date.

BofAML US Treasury Current 5 Year—Series of one-security indices in which the current "on-the-run" issue for each stated maturity remains in the index until the date a new one is auctioned and settles.

BofAML USD LIBOR 3 Month—Tracks interest rate at which banks can borrow funds, in marketable size, from other banks in the London interbank market. Fixed on a daily basis by the British Bankers' Association, it derives from a filtered average of the world's most creditworthy banks interbank deposit rates for larger loans with maturities between overnight and one full year.

BofAML USD LIBOR 3 Month EUR—Tracks an interest rate at which banks can borrow funds, in marketable size, from other banks in the London interbank market. Fixed on a daily basis by the British Bankers' Association, it derives from a filtered average of the world's most creditworthy banks interbank deposit rates for larger loans with maturities between overnight and one full year.

CBOE Buywrite Monthly—Benchmark index designed to reflect the return on a portfolio consisting of a long position in the stocks in the S&P 500 Index and a short position in an S&P 500 (SPX) call option.

CBOE S&P 500 Buywrite BXM—Benchmark Index designed to reflect the return on a portfolio that consists of a long position in the stocks in the S&P 500 Index and a short position in an S&P 500 (SPX) call option.

Citi Treasury Bill 1 Month—Measures monthly return equivalents of yield averages that are not marked to market. The One-Month Treasury Bill Index consists of the last one-month Treasury bill issue.

Citi Treasury Bill 3 Month—Measures monthly return equivalents of yield averages that are not marked to market. The Three-Month Treasury Bill Indices consist of the last three three-month Treasury Bill issues.

Citi WGBI NonUSD—Includes the 18 government bond markets of Australia, Austria, Belgium, Canada, Denmark, Finland, France, Germany, Greece, Ireland, Italy, Japan, the Netherlands, Portugal, Spain, Sweden, Switzerland, and the United Kingdom. It excludes the United States.

Dow Jones Brookfield Global Infrastructure—Measures the stock performance of companies that exhibit strong infrastructure characteristics. Index components are required to have more than 70% cash derived from infrastructure lines of business. The index measures all sectors of the infrastructure market.

Credit Suisse Convertible Arbitrage—Subset of the Credit Suisse Hedge Fund index that measures the aggregate performance of risk arbitrage funds. Risk arbitrage event-driven hedge funds typically attempt to capture the spreads in merger or acquisition transactions involving public companies after the terms of the transaction have been announced.

Credit Suisse Event Driven—Subset of the Credit Suisse Hedge Fund index that measures the aggregate performance of risk arbitrage funds. Risk arbitrage event-driven hedge funds typically attempt to capture the spreads in merger or acquisition transactions involving public companies after the terms of the transaction have been announced.

Credit Suisse Hedge Fund—Asset-weighted hedge fund index compiled by Credit Suisse Hedge Index LLC and CME Group Index Services LLC which includes only funds as opposed to separate accounts. The index uses the Credit Suisse Hedge Fund Database which tracks approximately 8,000 funds and consists only of funds with a minimum of $50 million under management, a 12-month track record, and audited financial statements. The index is calculated and rebalanced on a monthly basis and reflects performance net of all hedge fund component performance fees and expenses.

Credit Suisse Managed Futures—Measures the aggregate performance of managed futures funds (often referred to as CTAs or Commodity Trading Advisors) that typically focus on investing in listed bond, equity, commodity futures and currency markets, globally. Managers tend to employ systematic trading programs that rely largely upon historical price data and market trends.

Dow Jones Industrial Average—Represents large and well-known U.S. companies, covering all industries with the exception of Transportation and Utilities.

Dow Jones Moderate—Total-portfolio index that allows investors to evaluate the returns on their portfolios considering the amount of risk they have taken. The profiles are defined based on incremental levels of potential risk relative to the risk of an all-stock index. This index measures the performance of a portfolio with approximately 60% of the potential risk of an all-stock portfolio.

Dow Jones Moderately Aggressive—Total-portfolio index that allows investors to evaluate the returns on their portfolios considering the amount of risk they have taken. The profiles are defined based on incremental levels of potential risk relative to the risk of an all-stock index. This index measures the performance of a portfolio with approximately 80% of the potential risk of an all-stock portfolio.

Dow Jones Moderately Conservative—Total-portfolio index that allows investors to evaluate the returns on their portfolios considering the amount of risk they have taken. The profiles are defined based on incremental levels of potential risk relative to the risk of an all-stock index. This index measures the performance of a portfolio with approximately 40% of the potential risk of an all-stock portfolio.

Dow Jones UBS Commodity—Provides a broadly diversified representation of commodity markets as an asset class. The index is made up of exchange-traded futures on 19 physical commodities which are weighted to account for economic significance and market liquidity. Weighting restrictions on individual commodities and commodity groups promote diversification.

Dow Jones US Consumer Service—Measures the performance of U.S. stocks in the Consumer Services sector of the Dow Jones U.S. index as defined by the proprietary classification system used by Dow Jones indices.

Dow Jones US Contrarian Opportunities—Transparent, rules-based tool for benchmarking contrarian investment strategies designed to systematically measure the performance of stocks that lag behind the broader market in terms of recent performance but outrank their peers based on fundamentals-based and other qualitative criteria.

Dow Jones US Financial—Measures the performance of U.S. stocks in the Financials sector of the Dow Jones U.S. index as defined by the proprietary classification system used by Dow Jones indices.

Dow Jones US Health Care—Measures the performance of U.S. stocks in the Health Care sector of the Dow Jones U.S. index as defined by the proprietary classification system used by Dow Jones indices.

Dow Jones US Oil & Gas—Measures the performance of U.S. stocks in the Oil & Gas sector of the Dow Jones U.S. index as defined by the proprietary classification system used by Dow Jones indices.

Dow Jones US Select Dividend—Measures the performance of the country's leading stocks by dividend. One hundred stocks are selected to the index by dividend yield, subject to screens for dividend-per-share growth rate, dividend payout, ratio, and average daily dollar trading volume. Components are weighted by indicated annual dividend.

Dow Jones US Technology—Measures the performance of U.S. stocks in the Technology sector of the Dow Jones U.S. Index as defined by the proprietary classification system used by Dow Jones indices.

Dow Jones US Telecom—Measures the performance of U.S. stocks in the Telecommunications sector of the Dow Jones U.S. index as defined by the proprietary classification system used by Dow Jones indices.

FTSE EPRA/NAREIT Developed Ex US—Measures the performance of REITs listed in developed markets outside the U.S.

FTSE EPRA/NAREIT Developed—Tracks the performance of listed real estate companies and REITS worldwide. By making the index constituents free-float adjusted, liquidity-, size- and revenue-screened, the series is suitable for use as the basis for investment products such as derivatives and Exchange-Traded Funds (ETFs).

FTSE Gold Mines—Reflects the performance of the worldwide market in the shares of companies whose principal activity is the mining of gold. It is intended to supply gold investors and analysts with an accurate reflection and comprehensive coverage of the global gold markets. The index series encompasses all gold mining companies that have a sustainable and attributable gold production of at least 300,000 ounces a year, and that derive 51% or more of their revenue from mined gold.

FTSE World—Free-float market capitalization-weighted index. FTSE World Indices include components of the Large- and Mid-capitalization universe for Developed and Emerging Market segments.

HFRX Absolute Return—Representative of the overall composition of the hedge fund universe, it comprises all eligible hedge fund strategies including convertible arbitrage, distressed securities, equity hedge, equity market neutral, event-driven, macro, merger arbitrage, and relative value arbitrage. As a component of the optimization process, the index selects constituents that characteristically exhibit lower volatilities and lower correlations to standard directional benchmarks of equity market and hedge fund industry performance.

HFRX Aggregate—Equally weighted index across all substrategy and regional indices.

HFRX Equity Market Neutral—Represents the universe of Equity Market Neutral hedge funds. Equity Market Neutral strategies employ sophisticated quantitative techniques of analyzing price data to ascertain information about future price movement and relationships between securities and select securities for purchase and sale. These strategies typically maintain characteristic net equity market exposure no greater than 10%, long or short.

JPM CEMBI Broad Diversified—Tracks U.S. dollar-denominated debt issued by emerging market corporations. It includes fixed, floating, amortizing, and capitalizing instruments.

JPM CEMBI Diversified IG—Tracks U.S. dollar-denominated debt issued by emerging market corporations.

JPM EMBI Global—Tracks total returns for traded external debt instruments in the emerging markets, including U.S. dollar-denominated Brady bonds, loans, and Eurobonds with an outstanding fact value of at least $500 million.

JPM GBI EM Global Diversified—Tracks returns for actively traded local currency debt instruments issued by a selection of emerging market countries.

Morningstar Long-Only Commodity—Fully collateralized commodity futures index that is long all eligible commodities.

Morningstar Moderate Target Risk—Represents a portfolio of global equities, bonds, and traditional inflation hedges such as commodities and TIPS. This portfolio is held in a static allocation appropriate for U.S. investors who seek average exposure to equity market risk and returns.

MSCI AC Asia Ex Japan—Free-float adjusted market capitalization-weighted index that is designed to measure the equity market performance of Asia, excluding Japan, consisting of the following 10 developed and emerging market country indices: China, Hong Kong, India, Indonesia, Korea, Malaysia, Philippines, Singapore, Taiwan, and Thailand.

MSCI ACWI Ex USA—Free-float adjusted market capitalization-weighted index designed to measure the equity market performance of developed and emerging markets other than the U.S.

MSCI ACWI—Capturing large- and mid-cap representation across 24 developed and 21 emerging markets countries with over 2,500 constituents, the index covers approximately 84% of the global investable equity opportunity set.

MSCI ACWI Small Cap—Includes over 6,400 securities across 24 developed and 21 emerging markets.

MSCI China—Provides coverage of the large- and mid-cap segments constructed according to the MSCI Global Investable Market Indices methodology, and part of the MSCI Emerging Markets index.

MSCI EAFE Growth—Measures the performance of stocks in European, Australasian, and Far Eastern markets that represent growth characteristics.

MSCI EAFE—Free-float adjusted market capitalization index that is designed to measure the equity market performance of developed markets, excluding the U.S. and Canada.

Index

Numerics

.44 Magnum Leveraged Financing Program, 101
2 and 20, 110
7Twelve Portfolio, 79-80
401(k), 15
130/30 fund strategy, 128-129
2012 Global Survey on Alternative Investing, 62

A

absolute return, 71, 93
accredited investors, 109
advisory fees, 110
alternative investments, 4, 60-66
    10 important ponts, 159-161
    2012 Global Survey on Alternative Investing, 62
    adoption by institutional investors, 61-62
    arbitrage, 83-86
        currency arbitrage trading, 84
        merger arbitrage, 84-86
        relative value, 149-151
    corporate governance, 119
    disruption, 5
    due diligence, assessing, 103-104
    endowments, 6
    hedge funds, 135-139
        2 and 20, 110
        multi-strategy, 155
        regulations, 109-110
    investment reasoning, 119
    liquidity, 141-142
    partnerships, 139-141
        limited partnerships, 140-141
    private placements, 102
    public securities, 65
    trading strategies, 148
    variable annuities, 120-121
        annuity contracts, 120
        investment basis, 120
Andreessen, Marc, 158
Android operating system, 96
annuity contracts, 120
arbitrage, 83-86
    black boxes, 84
    convertible bond arbitrage, 150
    currency arbitrage trading, 84
    fixed-income arbitrage, 150-151
    merger arbitrage, 84-86
    relative value, 149-151
ARPANET (Advanced Research Projects Agency Network), 158
Asian Flu, 32
assessing due diligence, 103-104
asset allocation, 51
    tactical asset allocation, 118-119
asset classes
    correlation, 160
    growth of alternative asset classes, 112
    for nine-box investment strategies, 93-95

asset management companies, 37
availability of communication technology, 34

B

Baby Boomer generation, 16
balanced portfolios, 80
behavioral finance, 44
    prospect theory, 44-46, 69
benefit plans, 14-15
Bernanke, Ben, 2
beta, 78, 81-83. *See also* risk
beta blockers, 78
black boxes, 84
bonds, 26
    convertible bond arbitrage, 150
    "tapering," 61
    two-asset investment model, 80
    yield, 95-97
borrowed capital, leverage, 161
Botein, Matt, x
Bretton Woods monetary system, 33
Bull Durham, 68
Bush, George W., 2
buy-and-hold investing, 27, 118

C

calculating future cash flows, 95
CBOE (Chicago Board Options Exchange) Volatility Index, 22
Clark, James, 158
Cliffwater LLC, 142
Coca-Cola, 48
combining risk and return potential, 117-118
communication technology, availability of, 34
comparing hedge funds and mutual funds, 136

consulting investment professionals, 38-40
contribution plans, 15
convergence trading, 137
convertible bond arbitrage, 150
corporate governance, 119
corporate restructuring, 137
correlation, 36, 46-50, 146
    beta, 81-83
    positive correlation, 46
    two-asset investment model, 80
    between U.S and international markets, 47
Costner, Kevin, 68
credit default swaps, 34-35
The Crimson Permanent Assurance, 139
currency arbitrage trading, 84
cyclical nature of markets, 20-25
    interest rates, 23-25
    volatility, 29

D

deleveraging, 39
derivatives, 130
developed nations, market performance compared to emerging markets, 38-39
disruption, 5
distressed securities, 152
diversification, 17, 28
    7Twelve Portfolio, 79
    asset allocation, 51
    balanced portfolios, 80
    correlation, 36, 46-50
        positive correlation, 46
        between U.S and international markets, 47
    Enron bankruptcy, 45-46
    "home country bias," 37

international allocation, 37
risk parity, 86-87
risks, 52
two-asset investment model, 80
Wellington Fund, 79

Dow 36,000: The New Strategy for Profiting from the Coming Rise in the Stock Market (Glassman), 1

Dow Jones Industrial Average, 1
volatility, 7

Dresdner Financial, 101

due diligence, 101-105
assessing, 103-104
methods of performing, 104-105

Dychtwald, Dr. Ken, 14

E

emerging markets
hedge funds, 154
mutual funds, 65
performance compared to developed nations, 38-39

The Endowment Model, 58

endowments, 6, 28
shift to equities, 113
Yale University, 57

Enron bankruptcy, 45-46

equity long-short strategy, 152-153

equity-based asset classes, 93

evaluating investment managers, 118-119

event-driven investment strategies, 151-152

F

"fear index," 22

Federal Reserve Bank of New York, 33

financial communication, 34

financial crises and leverage, 130

financial professionals, advisory fees, 110

five-star rating system (Morningstar), 102

fixed-income arbitrage, 150-151

"flash crashes," 35, 160

"The Flu Game," 90

Frank, Barney, 2

frontier markets, 64

fund of funds, 141

future cash flows, calculating, 95

futures contracts, 129

G

GDP, growth of developing countries, 64

Generation Buy and Hold, 4

Glassman, James, 1

global macro investment strategy, 153-154

globalization, 29, 33-40
Asian Flu, 32
availability of communication technology, 34
Bretton Woods monetary system, 33
emerging market performance versus developed nations, 38-39
interconnectedness, 35
international allocation, 37

Goodyear Tire and Rubber Company, partnership with NASA, 56

Google, 96

Gore, Al, 158

Great Crash of 1929, 130

growth of GDP in developing countries, 64

H

Hassett, Kevin, 1
hedge funds, 109-111, 134-139, 161
  2 and 20, 110
  convergence trading, 137
  corporate restructuring, 137
  emerging markets, 154
  Long-Term Capital Management, 33
  management's investment objective, 139
  market directional hedge funds, 137
  multi-strategy, 155
  versus mutual funds, 136
  opportunistic hedge funds, 138
  private placement, 109
  regulations, 109-110
Hedge Funds Consistency Index, 149
high-water marks, 110
"home country bias," 36-37

I

importance of planning investments, 158
indices, 4
  correlation, 49
  Journal of Indexes, 74
  Standard and Poor's 100 Index, 22
  VIX, 22
inflation risk, 68
inflation-based asset classes, 93
institutional investors, 56
  adoption of alternative investment strategies, 61
interconnectedness, impact on volatility, 34-35

interest rates, 23-25
  bonds, 24, 26
  risk, 61
  yield, 95
international allocation, 37
International Monetary Fund, 33
intervals, 111
investing as art, 60
investment basis, 120
investment reasoning, 119
Isrealsen, Craig, 74, 79

J-K

Jackson, Phil, 100
Jordan, Michael, 90
Journal of Indexes, 74
Kahneman, Daniel, 44, 69
Kirtsaeng, Supap, 83
Knight Capital, 36

L

legislation, Revenue Act of 1978, 15
leverage, 126, 161
  130/30 fund strategy, 128-129
  .44 Magnum Leveraged Financing Program, 101
  deleveraging, 39
  derivatives, 130
  and financial crises, 130
  futures contracts, 129
  impact on mortgage industry, 127
  maintenance margin, 129
  misuse of, 127
  ultra funds, 130-131
Licklider, J.C.R., 158
limited partnerships, 140-141
Lipper, 93, 129
liquidity, 141-142

living benefit riders, 120
long security position, 128
longevity, impact on retirement, 14
Long-Term Capital Management, 33
loss aversion, 69-71
   sequence of return risk, 72-75
Lunn, Geoffrey, 101

M

maintenance margin, 129
Malone, Karl, 90
managing risk, beta, 81-83
market crash of 2008, 25-26
market directional hedge funds, 137
market neutral strategy, 153
markets
   cyclical nature of, 20-25
   globalization, 32
Markowitz, Harry, 3, 10
Martin, Andy, 79
Massachusetts Investors Trust, 62
McKinsey and Company, 111-112
medicine, effect on life expectancy, 11
merger arbitrage, 84-86, 151
Merton, Robert, 33
misuse of leverage, 127
mitigating risk, 68-69
   loss aversion, 69-71
   sequence of return risk, 72-75
money managers
   due diligence, 104
   evaluating, 118-119
Morgan, Walter, 79
Morningstar, 49
   five-star rating system, 102
   Style Box strategy, 91-92

mortgage industry, leverage, 127
Mosaic, 158
MPT (Modern Portfolio Theory), 10
   risk, 58-60
MSCI EAFE, 47
multi-manager investments, 141
multi-strategy hedge funds, 155
mutual funds
   emerging markets, 65
   five-star rating system (Morningstar), 102
   versus hedge funds, 136
   Massachusetts Investors Trust, 62
   public securities, 65
   selection process, Style Box strategy, 91-92
   top performers, 103
   Wellington Fund, 79

N

NASA, partnership with Goodyear, 56
NASDAQ, 36
Netscape, 158
Newman, Paul, 116
nine-box investment strategies, 93-95

O-P

opportunistic hedge funds, 138
optimizing portfolios, 117-118, 122
overlay management, 122-123
partnerships, 139-141
Patton, George S., 146
Paulson, John, 134
pension plans, 15
performing due diligence, 104-105
Pintaric, David, 116-117

Pioneering Portfolio Management (Swenson), 57
portfolios
   7Twelve Portfolio, 79
   alternative investments, adding, 51-52
   asset allocation, 51
   beta, 81-83
   diversification, 28
   optimizing, 117-118, 122
   overlay management, 122-123
   risk parity, 86-87
   selection process, Style Box strategy, 91-92
positive correlation, 46
private equity, 139
   limited partnerships, 140-141
   partnerships, 139-141
private placements, 102
   hedge funds, 109
prospectuses, 121
prospect theory, 44-46, 69
psychology, behavioral finance, 44
   prospect theory, 45-46
public securities, 65

Q-R

Quotron system, 34
Ramirez, Alberto, 127
Ramirez, Rosa, 127
Regulation D, 109
regulations for hedge funds, 109-110
REITs (real estate investment trusts), 103-104
relative return, 71
relative value, 149-151
   convertible bond arbitrage, 150
   fixed-income arbitrage, 150-151

resale value, 95
retirement plans, 14
   contribution plans, 15
   Social Security, 16
return approaches, 71
Revenue Act of 1978, 15
risk, 68, 75
   arbitrage
      currency arbitrage trading, 84
      merger arbitrage, 84-86
   beta, 78, 81-83, 87
   combining with return potential, 117-118
   in diversification, 52
   inflation risk, 68
   interest rates, 61
   loss aversion, 69-71
   mitigating, 68-69
   MPT, 58-60
   prospect theory, 69
   sequence of return risk, 72-75
risk parity, 86-87
Russell 3000, 47

S

Samsung, 48
SARS (Severe Acute Respiratory Syndrome) epidemic of 2003, 32
Scholes, Myron, 33
Scott, George C., 146
SEC, Regulation D, 109
secular patterns, 22
selecting investment strategies, 146-149
   arbitrage
      convertible bond arbitrage, 150
      fixed-income arbitrage, 150-151
   equity long-short strategy, 152-153

event-driven strategies, 151-152
global macro strategy, 153-154
sequence of return risk, 72-75
short security position, 128
short selling, 153
signs of underperforming investments, 118-119
Social Security, 16
Soros, George, 154
sovereign debt crisis, 27
Standard and Poor's (S&P) 100 Index, 22
stocks
   resale value, 95
   yield, 95-97
Stockton, John, 90
strategies for investments, selecting, 146-149
   arbitrage
      convertible bond arbitrage, 150
      fixed-income arbitrage, 150-151
   equity long-short strategy, 152-153
   event-driven strategies, 151-152
   global macro strategy, 153-154
Style Box strategy, 91-92
Swenson, David, 57-60, 83
Swenson's Asset Allocations, 59
Swenson's Sweet Spot, 57-58

T

tactical asset allocation, 118-119
Takahashi, Dean, 58
"tapering," 61
technology, dependence of investments on, 36
ThinkAdvisor.com, 61
timeshares, 110-111
   intervals, 111

trading strategies, 148
traditional investments, 36
transparency, 142
Tversky, Amos, 44
two-asset investment model, 80

U

ultra funds, 130-131
underperforming investments, signs of, 118-119
university endowments, 6
unpredictability of the market, 22

V

variable annuities, 120-121
   annuity contracts, 120
   investment basis, 120
VIX (CBOE Volatility Index), 22
volatility, 5, 160
   Asian Flu, 32
   beta, 78, 81-83
   cyclical volatility, 22, 29
   emerging market performance versus developed nations, 38-39
   "flash crash," 35
   interconnectedness, 34-35
   interdependencies, 34
   interest rates, 23-25
   market crash of 2008, 25-26
   VIX, 22

W

websites
   Hedge Funds Consistency Index, 149
   ThinkAdvisor.com, 61
Wellington Fund, 79
Wilson, Quentin, 10
World Bank, 33
WRP Investments, 116

X-Y-Z

Yale Investments Office, 113
The Yale Model, 58
Yale University, 57
yield, 95-97
   calculating future cash flows, 95
Zuckerman, Gregory, 134